K-9 KOREA

KOREA

THE UNTOLD STORY
OF AMERICA'S
WAR DOGS IN THE
KOREAN WAR

J. RACHEL REED

REGNERY
HISTORY

Regnery History™ is a trademark of Salem Communications Holding Corporation; Regnery® is a registered trademark of Salem Communications Holding Corporation

ISBN 978-1-62157-467-5

Cataloging-in-Publication Data on file with the Library of Congress

Published in the United States by
Regnery History
An imprint of Regnery Publishing
A Division of Salem Media Group
300 New Jersey Ave NW
Washington, DC 20001
www.RegneryHistory.com

Manufactured in the United States of America

10 9 8 7 6 5 4 3 2 1

Books are available in quantity for promotional or premium use. For information on discounts and terms, please visit our website: www.Regnery.com.

Distributed to the trade by
Perseus Distribution
www.perseusdistribution.com

CONTENTS

For Steve
Soldier, Dog Lover, and
the Best Daddy That Ever Lived

FOREWORD

On graduation day, the new graduates of the 8125th Sentry Dog Detachment stand ready for their assignment.

Even after fifty-nine years of separation, the men, more like brothers than friends, longed to be together again. Their time in Korea had been difficult and they hadn't always enjoyed each other's company, but time spent together in hell had bonded them like nothing else could. They had survived "The Forgotten War" and come home to a largely uncaring world—no hero's parade, no fanfare. But in many ways, they had never returned—they had left half of themselves in Korea.

Fickes strummed on his ukulele and sang, "Has anybody seen my gal?" The ladies in the room, wives and widows of the men, sang along. In another corner, Hatch finished telling an off-color joke. Everyone laughed; some slapped a knee and others wheezed from laughing too hard, likely the effect of many years of smoking. Their familiar interactions illustrated a kinship that had lasted through the years. Their time apart had not diminished their brotherhood.

Their songs and jokes were relics of that long-past time when distractions were a necessity; even in the worst situations of war, their camaraderie had always been a great comfort. And in those distant days on faraway soil, even the dogs had enjoyed the music and laughter. It had provided a welcome break in the monotony for both man and canine alike.

The fifty-ninth reunion of the 8125th Sentry Dog Detachment in Korea met, with the painfully apparent absence of some beloved members, as it had for the past nine years. There were no schedules or tours. The men, greying versions of their younger soldier selves, sat in their hotel suite soaking up the fellowship they had been deprived of for too long. Of the roughly sixty men who had served with the 8125th in Korea between 1954 and 1955, thirty-eight remained. Many had already passed away.

For many years I had been researching the role dogs play in war, and it was these stories of bravery and loyalty that kept me scouring news footage and archives with fervor. But it was when I stumbled on a small blurb about a group of Korea Vets, Army dog handlers from the 8125th, holding an annual reunion in Colorado Springs, that I found the best untold stories I had ever known. Fred Batson was pictured in the *Colorado Gazette* story, and his daughter Rhonda Batson was quoted in the text. A preliminary search for Fred Batson yielded nothing, but I was able to find Rhonda. I reached out to her, and she offered to connect me to Fred. I jumped at the offer and called him right away.

This is how I became the honorary oddball member of the group. During our introductory phone call, Batson asked me if I would be interested in coming to the next year's reunion and listening to their "old stories." Of course, following old soldiers around and listening to them talk about the dogs they loved in war sounded like my idea of a perfect evening, but greater still, the mystery of the unit's story was a puzzle I felt compelled to solve. I wondered why I had never heard of the unit in all of my previous research. I couldn't understand why prominent war dog histories had made no mention of sentry dogs in Korea. The men of the 8125th had become ghosts, and the dogs were invisible. I would be chasing shadows, but shadows that I knew needed to be caught.

So I came (in retrospect, a bit naïve), my iPad in hand, along with an empty notebook, and a brand new pack of pens. I was ready to hear anything, and I was going to do my best to capture every detail. I had no idea that the joy on the surface of this reunion of veterans masked a seething tragedy—one each of the men felt keenly.

The question that had weighed heavily on their hearts since their return to the United States in 1955 was "Why?"

Why did their country forget them while they were away? Why did the Department of the Army tell them that their dogs—not just dogs to them but beloved fellow soldiers, their most loyal companions, their greatest friends—would return home with them at war's end when it was all a lie?

The intervening years had brought no good answers, but these reunions had made life easier for the men. Every man there had returned home to a seemingly indifferent nation. Every man there had been forced to leave his dog behind. Yet these reunions transcended that pain, if only for a short time, by becoming the glue which held them together.

Their canine partners had been more than just tools of the trade. Soldier and K-9 were equals, and their bond went much deeper than anyone outside the division could understand.

By end of the evening, in our little hotel suite overlooking the Colorado River, I had recorded the men's recollections as best as I could, working carefully to get every last detail since I had no way of knowing when or if I would see the aging group again. I had resigned myself to the bitter conclusion that the dogs had all been lost. Time had forgotten them and history had recorded it inaccurately. Their tragic story was not unlike that of the Korean conflict as a whole, with the unit's contributions relegated to a single sentence, if that, in the voluminous history of America's wars. Worse still, the dogs, once promised a return home at the end of the rotation, never made it back. At least now we had the opportunity to set the record straight. The dignity earned by both man and dog had been denied far too long, and the weight to tell that story now rested on my shoulders.

I packed up my things, reluctant to tear myself away from this wonderful group of friends. The men, the spouses, and the widows had all been generous in pouring out their hearts to me; their faith in me, to get their story out to the world, was immense—how could I not deliver what needed to be told? The men and dogs of the 8125th served their country with unwavering devotion. What set their story apart, however, was their loyalty and devotion to each other. The men had formed a lifelong fraternity, and each dog and man team had formed such a unique bond that it could, in many cases, be described as life-changing. Aren't we as a society better, stronger, when we have these best examples of humanity to rest our hopes on? And aren't we better when we can look at the failures of humanity and vow, "Never again"?

I knew I had my own duty now. If I followed my heart in writing this story, then it would honor the valiant efforts of real men and their beloved canine partners. If I wrote this story from my gut, the world would understand a great injustice so that it might become a part of our collective memory and never happen again.

PROLOGUE

When I first met the men of the 8125th at their fifty-ninth reunion, they welcomed me by throwing an ID badge around my neck and hugging me like the prodigal daughter. They had made my badge to match their own. Each man carried a picture of his dog to identify him. My dog was Chief. Of course, Chief had been Wooden's dog, but he was a symbol of the power, ferocity, and loyalty that all the dogs possessed. He was also their symbol of loss. In a way, Chief was America's dog. He stood on the edge of the night and watched. He had died a hero's death, a super hero who made sure that someone's beloved son made it home alive. I took my badge in reverence.

It was Harlan's first time at a reunion too. He had been looking for anyone associated with 8125th, hoping to find the guys he had served with, but had found the guys from this later rotation instead.

I thought I might have a fellow freshman to tag along with. Although he made me feel beyond welcomed, he also proved to be more senior than new guy. His stories about his time in Korea before the other men had arrived provided missing pieces to puzzles long unsolved. He gave some history on certain dogs and explained why many things played out the way they had for the other guys. His shenanigans were relatable, too, as soldiers seem to find the same ways, even across the ages, to entertain themselves and blow off steam. Another common thread between Harlan and the other men was his deep admiration for his dog, Greta—the same undeniable bond between soldier and dog that the rest of us can never comprehend, although we admire it.

Simpson told me about Broadway and Blind Sam, and I felt an instant love for Broadway, even though I hadn't met him yet. Simpson had pulled me aside and in a whisper, with tears in his eyes, told me, "One of the dogs lived a happy life with friends. One of the dogs lived!" I was pleasantly shocked. I wondered how these two men kept the secret of such a noble act for nearly sixty years. Simpson had never told a soul, only revealing it to me when he knew that Broadway couldn't be harmed by it, but would be honored instead. I found myself in a puddle of tears, admiring the love this group of men and dogs had shared.

I left the men of the 8125th on the last day of the reunion, vowing to remain in their lives forever. Their story had to be told. Their work had to be honored. The dogs needed a voice. History would mark their time with respect, and the dogs would live on in our collective memory.

1

WAR DOGS

WORLD WAR II

For as long as dogs have been man's best friends, they have accompanied men everywhere, even into war, bringing their own special set of skills to the fight. In the Stone Age, historical record shows, mastiff-type dogs fought alongside their human counterparts in Tibet. The ancient Persians, Greeks, and Babylonians all employed war dogs in battle.[1] More recently, in American history, dogs made their presence known in each one of our conflicts. During the American Revolution and the American Civil War, dogs took up residence in camps and followed soldiers across land for food and companionship. In World War I, dogs served their military masters by delivering messages across battle lines and by staying in foxholes to comfort shell-shocked warriors. Yet it wasn't until the horrors of

1

war came to our shores on Pearl Harbor Day that Americans began to consider dogs as both loyal companions and effective combat tools.

In the spirit of fully giving everything for the war effort during World War II, many American dog enthusiasts approached the Department of Defense about the possibility of developing war dogs for the coming combat needs. Kennel clubs across America understood the depths of canine talents and abilities. They had witnessed their obedience in the show ring and their demonstration of instinct in hunting trials that made America's canines an obvious asset to the U.S. military. Authorities on dog obedience and professional dog handlers met with the power players of the dog world, such as Harry Caesar, director of the American Kennel Club (AKC) in 1942, to develop a game plan for pitching our nation's first official Military Working Dog program. With the enthusiastic support of dog lovers President Franklin D. Roosevelt and his wife, Eleanor, and an overwhelming response from Americans willing to give anything to the war effort, Dogs for Defense (DFD) was established in January 1942.

Initially, Dogs for Defense was made up of an entirely voluntary force. Recruitment posters went up around the country touting the benefits of canine soldiers. Ads in major newspapers, magazines, and newsreels had a clear message: Dogs bring a capability to the fight that cannot be matched by man or machine. This was especially true of sentry dogs that could guard people and property by utilizing their alert barks, growls, and hackles, and had the ability to unleash a deadly attack when necessary. Further, their keen senses and highly developed perception at night could replace the efforts of six armed men.[2] As a result of this media blitz, Dogs for Defense was able to entice loving dog owners into donating their dogs to the cause. The thought of America's sons being freed up to do more valuable work was an idea fully supported nationwide.

As dogs began pouring in, however, a major problem arose for Army officials. There were no canine training facilities established, and no standard of training for the dogs. This was fine for many of the jobs for which dogs were needed, but for sentry dogs a specialized training was critical. These dog soldiers would require a natural prey-drive and aggression for protection and detection, while also possessing the smarts to temper those innate instincts, which were not always part of a donated dog's personality. Further, a soldier would have to be trained as a handler alongside his canine partner to tap into the dog's natural capabilities.

Realizing that the United States could effectively employ sentry dogs for the purpose of homeland security, and knowing this would require specialized training, Lieutenant Colonel Clifford Smith, a high-ranking officer in the U.S. Quartermaster Corps, discussed ways to make this training a reality with many of America's leading dog experts. On March 13, 1942, with authorization from his chain of command, Smith notified AKC Director Harry Caesar that Dogs for Defense would be run under the authority of the U.S. Quartermasters who would, from that time forward, be responsible for canine recruitment and training. This marked America's first official involvement in a military working dog program.

There was still no military breeding program in place, and the need for dogs (especially specific dog breeds notorious for aggression) was growing.[3] By the end of 1942, the call had been sent to America's dog enthusiasts and patriots: the Quartermaster Corps hoped to have 125,000 dogs in their ranks as quickly as possible.[4] Front Royal, Virginia, once home to cavalry stables and a prominent race track, became the first canine training and reception center for military working dogs. The U.S. Quartermaster recognized the facility at Front Royal as an institution with a renowned ability to handle horses, and believed that would easily translate into handling dogs. Subsequently other facilities popped up around the country, with the Marines and Coast Guard creating their own separate training centers to accommodate their individual needs.

Americans continued to answer the call by sending their beloved pets by the thousands, thereby creating another unexpected problem for Dogs for Defense. These families had raised their dogs from birth and saw them as family members. It was, for many, as if they were sending their own sons into battle. In the early stages of dog donation, no clear guidelines had been established about ownership of the dogs, and this started America's war dog program down a slippery slope. This situation, created by the indelible human-canine bond, would plague the nation's military throughout this and subsequent wars.

Mail flooded into the reception and training centers from across the country as people inquired about the welfare of their donated dogs. Trying not to reveal matters of operational security, the Department of Defense (DOD) sent return letters simply stating that their dogs had been received and were being cared for. This was the only official correspondence between the DOD and donating families. Many of the handlers, however, became incredibly attached to the dogs and wanted families back home to know that their dogs were loved and highly valued. Often service men would write to donating families, even from overseas, and keep them apprised of their dog's situation.

At the end of World War II, the U.S. military had not accounted for the relationships forged between soldiers and their dogs or the bonds between donating families and the dogs they had given. Many families back home expected that if their dog survived the war, it would be returned to them. Likewise handlers, not knowing what the regulations for returning dogs would be, hoped that they could take their military working dog home at the end of their service together. Then there was the occasional instance when a dog survived but had no one home looking forward to its return and no handler capable of keeping it. Americans overwhelmingly stepped in, just as they had to donate dogs to the war effort, to fill this need for loving adoptive homes.

By late 1945 Dogs for Defense had received over 15,000 applications, more than the number of dogs actually available.[5] Because DFD was begun by some of this country's most devoted dog lovers, the organization remained committed to the dogs they recruited. Dogs with no home were offered to Americans who were capable of caring for them.[6] Often this meant dogs with special needs arising from combat fatigue and aggression training would go to those experienced with the breed or with so-called "problem dogs." Any living creature that survives war will not return unscathed; many canines experienced severe post-traumatic stress and could not overcome their fearfulness of everyday situations. Some dogs had been trained as sentries and were therefore more aggressive than when they had left. In some isolated instances it was in the interest of the dog's welfare that they be humanely euthanized. For good measure, DFD also created a desensitization program before dogs were placed in civilian homes.

FRITZ

Fritz, a Doberman sentry dog who had been donated to the war effort, exemplified both the challenges and the successes of the Dogs for Defense transition program. Following World War II, he was rehomed with Hut Vass and his family.

In the years before World War II, Hut's grandmother had raised many dogs considered to be aggressive breeds. She had, in the years after her husband passed, witnessed the whelping of two German Shepherds, one American Pit Bull, and several Doberman Pinscher pups. These dogs were raised with rigorous expectations. Each must be aggressive enough to serve as personal protector to a lady, and gentle enough to be her constant companion. She loved these characteristics the most: brute strength and gentle submission. She also greatly admired the dogs' intellect and ability to discern when protection was necessary over play.

One of the Dobermans had been especially good at this job. He constantly watched Hut's grandmother, waiting for her to give some indication of where his protective services might be needed next. Every Sunday, without fail, she grabbed her Sunday hat signifying that they were going to church. In response, her beloved guardian would bolt out the back door, down the country lanes, into town, through the front doors of the Presbyterian church, and would end his run at "Grandmother's" pew. There in the aisle, he would wait for her to arrive by car for the Sunday service, and there he would lie by her side until the service had ended.[7]

On December 7, 1941, when Hut was just six years old, the Japanese attacked Pearl Harbor; there was no doubt in the American mind that the country was going to war. He could remember well his parents and grandmother listening to the radio program that announced the tragic attack on American soil. Even at a young age, Hut knew this meant the sacrifices would be great and much would be required of everyone. As his parents readied themselves, his grandmother made the suggestion Hut didn't want to hear: "We can send our dogs."

One of the family's young Dobermans had already set himself apart from the others by being a quick study. He had watched grandmother's Doberman and learned that guarding and protecting was what a dog like him was born to do. This young dog had taken to Hut, and had even worked his way out of the kennel and into Hut's bed. Every night Hut would go to sleep with the dog curled at his feet. Hut understood, deep down, that his dear canine friend was destined for war, and he cried at the thought of saying good-bye to his best buddy. But even at the age of six he understood the level of sacrifice necessary to win the war. He daydreamed about his dog defeating the whole Japanese Empire with one paw tied behind his back.

Both Hut's Doberman and his grandmother's canine companion were donated to the war effort—a difficult separation for everyone involved, but one they undertook with courage. In the years to follow, Hut's Danville, Virginia, community suffered many losses as young men went away, some of them never to return. The Vass family heard word through the grapevine that their dog was doing well, and one day they received confirmation by way of a letter from overseas. The dog's handler continued to send letters throughout the war, keeping them informed of the dog's well-being. He was never able to say where the K-9 team was stationed, only writing that they were "overseas." Yet one thing was clear: Hut's canine guardian had become a guardian to many and a true hero. He was proud of his dog for being every bit the soldier they knew he could be.

The family, however, did not realize the depth of the bond formed in war between handler and dog. Shortly after V-J Day, Hut's family received a different kind of letter than they had ever received before. It was a desperate plea from the handler, begging them to allow him to keep the military working dog that had become his closest comrade. Hamilton Vass, Hut's father, felt it was the right thing to do. Hut was devastated to learn that his parents had made the decision to let the handler keep the beloved dog, but his dad had explained that there were other dogs that needed their family more.

Hamilton had heard through friends (who were affiliated with the American Kennel Club) and fellow Doberman breeders that Dogs for Defense was looking for qualified homes to take in the sentry dogs who had survived the war. He knew that these dogs would be very challenging, but he also realized they were not lost causes but great dogs with special needs. Because of the family's experience with the breed, Hamilton also knew that their home was the best place for a Doberman. He hoped that another Doberman could bring Hut's grandmother peace after losing her beloved companion, and he believed Hut would benefit from a new friend. Without hesitation, Hamilton sent an adoption request to Dogs for Defense.

Fritz, a sixty-four-pound Doberman, came to the Vass home at the relatively young age of six. He had been given an "Honorable Discharge" from the Army Air Corps, and the family was given his certificate of such. No one knew for sure what Fritz had seen and done in his service, but they did know he had acted as sentry in Adak Island, Alaska.

During World War II Adak, one of the Aleutian Islands, was a key location for American troop placement in the Pacific and was intensely targeted by the Japanese. Few places required more of the extreme vigilance and keen senses of America's K-9s.

The Vass family understood that Fritz had served his post in Adak to the fullest and had saved countless American lives in the process. They also understood the fear he might have known from long, dark nights on patrol and the aggression he had to possess in order to protect his handler. A reporter from the *Danville Register Bee* came to talk with the Vass family about Fritz's retirement and described the dog's former training:

In addition to teaching the dog to obey his commands, the trainer must also instill in the dog the idea that every human, except himself, is his natural enemy. The dog is thus encouraged to alert when any stranger appears and to attempt to attack, despite the fact that he is kept on leash. The trainer must never allow another person to pet or make friends with the dog, keeping in mind that he himself is the only friend that the dog must know; he is the only master.[8]

It would seem, based on this account of a sentry dog's handling, that these dogs could never be rehabilitated. Hamilton knew Dobermans to be smart, however, and fiercely loyal above all, possessing boundless and forgiving love for people. Certainly Fritz might be more loving to one man than another, but Hamilton believed the desire for companionship and praise would override any aggression he had learned. Fritz had lost his constant companion of the past three years and that was the hardest life for any dog—a life without a master, and thus without love. Hamilton hated to see any dog face that despair. The family was willing to take a chance on Fritz.

Hut, still reeling from the pain of an unfulfilled reunion with his own dog, hoped Fritz might take his Doberman's place at the foot of his bed, and he was disappointed to find that would never be possible because of the dog's aloof demeanor. Probably due to the military life Fritz had led, he was slow to warm up to Hut and seemed to have a problem with children in general. Once Fritz lunged with full force at a boy in town who pulled out a pop gun from the waistband of his jeans. Fortunately, he had been on a leash and under Hamilton's control at the time.

For general safety Fritz remained on leash when in public for the rest of his life. At the farm however, Fritz was given free rein, and he took the opportunity to be a dog whenever he could. In his retirement he adored chasing rabbits, doing so with wild abandon. This is where Hut finally made a connection with Fritz, because he loved running those Virginia hills right alongside him. And over the years, the family found one thing that Fritz adored even more, a love which was rooted in the very nature of a Doberman. He lived to protect, and he needed an outlet for his unending devotion. He found his purpose with Hut's grandmother.

POST-WAR AND KOREA

In 1946, the U.S. Quartermaster stopped accepting donated dogs into their military working dog program. This was not the end of the practice of using military working dogs but a drawdown of canine forces and a way of obtaining the best possible working dogs for the task. It was also a somewhat feeble attempt at addressing the problem of ownership and the bonds that naturally exist between people and the dogs they make their companions. Instead of relying on private citizens to give their pets away, the military would undertake a purchase program to buy the best examples of the desired breed from private breeders.[9] This was a method the military had effectively employed throughout the country's history with horses and mules, and they believed it would make the question of "ownership" less problematic. Further, in the post-war years, military officials couldn't envision a future need for the various types of dogs used in World War II. They didn't foresee another war on the scale of World War II and didn't believe there was a need, in the immediate future, which would justify the cost of maintaining a war dog program. They planned to refine the process to include only German Shepherds, which had proved to be the most effective breed for the military's purposes.

Initially scout dogs, known for their ability to track down the enemy in advance of troops, were seen as largely unnecessary in a post-World War II world, in spite of their proven effectiveness in saving lives. Yet many senior military advisors warned against dropping the ball on preparedness, especially in regard to the nation's incredibly effective canine program.[10] Brigadier General Frederick McCabe advised the U.S. Quartermaster in 1946 to keep a war dog program in place and to expand training and breeding programs for scouts and sentries. Ultimately his recommendations were not fully realized, and there remained only a tiny group of scout dogs in America's arsenal.[11] Although they would bounce from post to post in the years leading up to the Korean conflict, the Twenty-Sixth Infantry Scout Dog Platoon became America's go-to canine corps in Korea.

The Twenty-Sixth moved from Front Royal, Virginia, to Fort Riley, Kansas, in 1948, two years before America entered the Korean conflict with full military involvement. As the "conflict" intensified, the U.S. military began to see the potential for a quagmire. As early as 1951, the seemingly endless, brutal, and bloody battles in Korea had reached a stalemate. Meanwhile, back home, many American people were turning a blind eye to American servicemen and their efforts on the Korean peninsula. Collectively, the nation seemed to find it difficult to stomach the idea of another extended U.S. military engagement.[12] American generals on the ground in Korea, on the other hand, knew that in order to push beyond the stalemate at the Thirty-Eighth Parallel, there must be a full commitment of forces. Remembering the effectiveness of America's K-9 units in World War II, they turned once again to the dogs.

The Twenty-Sixth Scout Dog Platoon was a small contingent of roughly six dogs and six handlers and a young Lieutenant OIC (officer in charge). In the spring of 1951 they were called up and, upon their arrival in Korea, readily welcomed by the battle-tested Second Infantry Division. Many soldiers attached to the Second were comforted by the presence of the dogs in the Twenty-Sixth. Dogs are not only remarkable sniffers and the most amazing detecting devices; they are also deeply comforting in their nature. To see a dog in war or even better, to touch a dog, is a powerful and tangible reminder of home and better days. The Twenty-Sixth scouts proved effective on the front lines in Korea and were even awarded for their meritorious service, but perhaps their most important contribution to the war effort was their positive effect on the morale of beat-down GIs. How much the dogs' emotional support made life more bearable for many living in the war zone was never fully appreciated by military officials.[13]

MORALE DOGS

The comfort soldiers receive from dogs in war has historically been under-appreciated by military officials, but ask any GI who has ever had contact with one in the war zone and he will tell you: dogs are some of the very best morale builders around.

Perhaps military officials worried dogs were a distraction—in some ways, they were certainly right. Yet the type of distraction these four-legged companions offered was incredibly positive. In fact, dogs have consistently proven to be an effective means of psychological healing. The oral histories and photographs of returning veterans, for as long as there have been veterans, prove that dogs have been a comfort to many of the shell-shocked and battered.[14]

One argument the military maintained against befriending stray dogs in the war zone was that they could spread disease to military members and therefore pose a greater threat than benefit to the soldiers. The risk of rabies, especially in underdeveloped countries where rabies often ran rampant, could be quite high. On the other hand, the safe, effective, and inexpensive rabies vaccine for humans had been used for many years prior to our nation's involvement in Korea. It could easily have been argued that the vaccines should have been given to deploying troops anyway, since they were deploying to a region already rife with the disease. The risk of coming in contact with the disease from a rabid wild animal would be just as great as contracting it from a domestic dog or cat.

Ultimately there was no way to stop military members from seeking the comfort stray dogs offered in war. Countless times the animals were taken in as a company mascot or battle companion in total disregard for the wishes of those higher on the chain of command. Many soldiers, sailors, airmen, marines, and coastguardsmen were willing to take the chance. Still, on odd occasions stories surfaced of the highest ranking member in the chain of command not only condoning mascots, but even going so far as to encourage their presence. These commanders were remembered by their subordinates with great affection.

Even the compassionate commanders, however, were reluctant to make arrangements for morale dogs to be sent back to the United States once the war was over. In most cases, it could have been accomplished relatively easily by sending the dog aboard the homeward-bound ship with its adoptive soldier. This arrangement most likely wouldn't have cost the Department of Defense anything, and even if it did, the soldiers were willing to pick up the cost themselves. Unfortunately, such arrangements were seldom made. The soldiers who adopted dogs in Korea usually contented themselves with hoping the dog would be cared for by another soldier coming behind him. Knowing how much the dog had improved his own morale, a soldier was usually willing to live with the arrangement.

BENO

One such little dog, Beno, went from pathetic stray to beloved member of the United States Navy just by being himself.

A young sailor aboard the USS *Leyte* found a dog (or really, the dog found him) while in port in Yokosuka, Japan, and he couldn't leave him behind. The aircraft carrier had been headed for Korea in the summer of 1950 and allowed a brief R&R for the sailors en route. This young sailor had spent the afternoon exploring the port, mostly alone, but shadowed by one very cute, very persistent stray dog. No matter where the sailor went throughout the day, the dog would not be shaken.

In the evening, the sailor returned to the dock where he could catch a water taxi to the awaiting ship. The little dog followed. When he was discovered, the taxi driver told the sailor he was going to have to take the little dog aboard the awaiting ship because there was no way he was taking it back to the dock. The sailor looked at the driver and said, "That's not my dog."

His dog or not, the little dog followed the sailor up the gangplank and right to the OIC. When the OIC asked about the dog the sailor replied, "He's not my dog, he just follows me around. I can't stop him."

"He can't stay," the OIC explained. "He's got to go."

A higher ranking officer overheard the conversation and intervened. "He's a nice dog," the officer said. "I'm going over your head to the Old Man on this one." The little dog sat and looked on patiently.

And so it went, up the chain of command and right to the captain. The captain, being wise and knowing the positive effect a dog could have on everyone during an insufferably long deployment, commanded the junior officers to welcome the dog aboard.

From then on, the confident little dog went everywhere aboard ship, always at his sailor's side, but amenable to the love and snacks all the sailors offered. Collectively the men of the O-I Division decided his name should be "Beno," because for as long as he was aboard, there would "be no liberty and be no movies."

Kent Madenwald slept in the same berth compartment as the sailor and Beno. He remembered how much everyone loved the dog and would do anything just to be around him. The men made one bed for Beno in their sleeping compartment and another in the Combat Information Center (CIC) where they worked. The captain of *Leyte* made arrangements for Beno's food to be brought in by helicopter, a pallet load at a time. Madenwald also remembers that someone made Beno his very own uniform, a perfect replica of what the men wore. As far as the men were concerned, that scrappy little dog was "one of us."

By the end of operations in Korea, *Leyte* had been in service for 128 consecutive days. They were detached from the Seventy-Seventh Task Force and given orders to return home. Beno was to stay on board with his sailor, through the Panama Canal and beyond, until they had reached their final destination in Virginia Beach.

The entire *Leyte* crew was commended for their efforts during the Korean conflict, and Vice Admiral Struble came aboard to commend the captain and crew personally for their good work. A pinning ceremony was scheduled on deck, and Beno was, of course, in attendance. Unknown to Beno and all of his sailors, however, the admiral had heard of his good work as well. He had been the best morale boost the ship had ever seen, and for that Struble awarded Beno a "Good Sailor" certificate. Cheers went up aboard deck as Beno ran around barking and soaking up the festivities.

When Beno and his sailor docked in Virginia Beach, they walked off together and were never heard from again. Kent Madenwald was sure, however, that Beno had a good home with his sailor for the rest of his days. The bond between the two had become completely unbreakable and, regardless of circumstance, the dog would never leave the sailor's side. He also knew that Beno would live on in the hearts of all those sailors who served with him for the rest of their lives. They were thankful for Beno's very presence in those difficult days on the *Leyte*, and so very grateful for the joy he brought into their lives.[15]

SCHOSSI

In 1951, Leo Coe was a seventeen-year-old private attached to the First Cavalry Division, Seventh Regiment in Korea. He had been trained as a rifleman and as such had seen his share of action on the front lines. His unit had held their ground and then was based at a village south of Seoul called Yong Dong Po. In the summer of 1951, Leo was serving as a driver for officers at regiment headquarters. The Second Infantry Division had pulled back from their position north of Seoul and had come to Yong Dong Po to be re-equipped. This was the same summer that the U.S. Army decided to bring a small contingent of scout dogs into the fight. Top military officials knew that scout dogs had a way of penetrating lines that were otherwise impenetrable, thus alerting and protecting the lives of thousands of U.S. soldiers in one movement. When the Twenty-Sixth Scout Dog Platoon joined the Second Infantry Division in Korea in June 1951, they were a welcome sight to many.

Leo hadn't paid much attention to the various troop movements going on at Yong Dong Po, but he had noticed the scout dogs right away. They came in like celebrities, pursued by eager and adoring fans. Every time a handler walked down the road with a dog, or went into the mess with his dog, GIs swarmed the canine team for a closer look. Unable to break military discipline, many times the handler would have to deny a request to pet the dog. But if there was an opportunity, in a relaxed atmosphere away from the structured work life of a scout dog, the handler, knowing the redemptive power of his dog, would gladly allow it.

Leo had adopted a Korean mutt, Schossi, and he worried about his little dog breaking ranks and inviting the scout dogs to break the rules. Schossi was a clever dog. He had learned that attaching himself to an American post meant not only survival, but a pretty comfortable life as well. All that was ever required of him was to lie on soldiers' bunks and go for the occasional ride in a Jeep. In return he was kept safe and well-fed. In reality, he was just as much a lifesaver to the men as they had been for him. The men adored Schossi, and many said their lives were vastly improved just by being near him.

The Korean people were a starving and impoverished nation, and during the war years they were willing to eat just about anything—including dogs. Not that dog would have been offensive to them before. In fact, it was perfectly acceptable in Korean culture to eat dogs, but the millions of people living in famine throughout Asia during the war added an element of desperation. No living creature was off-limits to a hungry people, and dogs were some of the most plentiful meat available. In spite of that evolving threat, however, many dogs adapted in those difficult years and reverted back to a time when their ancestors could be both predator and prey. Dogs like Schossi found their survival in the hands of the Americans.

One day, not long after the Twenty-Sixth arrived at Yong Dong Po, Leo and Schossi had the unplanned opportunity to meet the scouts' OIC while the six dogs and handlers were out training. Seeing all the excitement of other dogs jumping barrels, sniffing the ground, and running out and back, Schossi had run into the scout dogs' training yard for a closer look. The scout dogs were intrigued but impeccably trained never to alert with excessive barking. Schossi, however, loved barking and he wanted to show the other dogs how it was done. He barked, danced, and wagged in delight.

Curious about the ruckus, the young lieutenant came out of the tent and eyeballed the little dog causing chaos in the ranks. Private Leo Coe feared severe disciplinary action for his dog's interference with government exercises. Coe yelled for Schossi to come back, but to no avail. The little dog was having the time of his life.

So Coe decided to make his apologies and plead for mercy instead. But as he walked toward the officer, the man knelt down and, with an opening motion of his arms, called the rambunctious little dog to his side. To Coe's relief, the young officer appeared almost jovial. Coe couldn't believe his luck.

Private and lieutenant exchanged military customs, the subordinate showing respect to the superior, but then they spoke about their love of dogs. It was a uniting moment for the two that allowed them to breech the conversation of home and family and the things they missed most. In the year that followed, Coe became the lieutenant's driver and the two became good friends. Schossi and the scout dogs became friends, too—or at least they had an understanding, dog to dog.

Coe had to leave Schossi behind when he left Korea. There was no way the military would allow for Schossi to travel with the unit. In a way it was painful to think of saying goodbye to this dog who had truly become his best friend. He feared that the good-natured Schossi might wander away from camp and into the wrong hands, but leaving him behind for the others wasn't a difficult choice at all. He knew that Schossi would be loved and cared for by his fellow soldiers. Leo also felt a sense of peace in knowing Schossi would be a lifeline to the many human brothers he left behind.

SENTRY DOGS IN KOREA

In spite of a lack of foresight on the part of U.S. military officials, the U.S. Army's scout dog program flourished throughout the Korean conflict. Due to the success of the Twenty-Sixth Infantry Scout Dog Platoon in battle, the Army felt it was necessary to continue training scout dogs for war. In December 1951, Army scout dog training moved again from Fort Riley, home of the first six scout dogs sent into Korea, to Camp Carson, Colorado. There they joined a contingent of Army sentry dogs which had recently been procured by the Army for another shot at making a war dog program. At the time, Camp Carson was training roughly eighty sentry dog handlers and nearly 400 dogs (sentry and scout dog prospects) in an eight-week training cycle.

The sentry dogs had endured through the military drawdown because of their effectiveness in protecting equipment and their ability to save money during World War II.[16] It was undeniable that sentry dogs were good for the bottom line. Moreover, sentry dogs, like scout dogs, could use their senses to protect lives. This mostly meant the lives of their handlers, but by stopping the enemy from infiltrating post perimeters, sentries undoubtedly thwarted many attacks and saved the lives of others as well.

Sentries had a reputation for being cold-blooded killers in war because of their attack training, and this is the main distinction between scouts and sentries. It was a by-product of the sentries' aggressive displays that they were also trained to do bite work. Where a scout dog needed to be stealthy, a sentry had to be showy. Yet there are very few cases of sentry dogs actually killing the enemy. Most often, it was the threat of a sentry's aggression—bearing fangs and raising hackles—which stopped would-be assailants.

The Army understood that both types of dog work were needed in Korea. For the first time in U.S. history, they had purchased dogs from private owners, thereby making them military equipment. The money and time invested in the dog and its training meant that dogs would no longer be returned if they didn't perform. Instead, the dogs that had come to Camp Carson for training would be utilized in one way or another. For instance, when a scout dog was an excessive barker, or showed a fear response with snapping and lunging, the kennel master would pass the dog on to the sentries. (It didn't work the other way around. Sentries could not become scouts, even when they couldn't show the level of aggression the military desired.) Seemingly, this one-size-fits-all policy came about because of a narrow military mindset which believed that so-called aggressive dogs were unable to be stealthy or amicable even to their handlers. Of course, this made the training of scouts and sentries in the same location a convenience for the Army, but it failed to take into consideration the suitability of the dogs for the jobs they were given.

Showing signs of aggression didn't always signify that a dog possessed a truly aggressive nature. Dogs that had been purchased from the public for sentry work, based on breed and conformation, weren't necessarily the vicious dogs they were supposed to be. The trainers at Camp Carson learned to teach the dogs aggressive behaviors, but they could never be sure if a dog behaved aggressively out of natural tendencies or to please its handler. The only sure way was to take a dog into the warzone and see how he performed. Once again, the U.S. military failed to address the obvious problem of using a living, breathing being as equipment, asking trainers to treat their dogs like machines. This was a recipe for disaster which would be fully realized in the years to come.

ADWIN

The story of Airman Robert O'Gara and his military working dog, Adwin, illustrates the disastrous results of categorizing an animal as equipment and man as a machine. O'Gara's heartbreak would continue to be military working dog handlers' tragic tale throughout the Korean conflict, and even in Vietnam.

In 1952, Robert O'Gara joined the Air Force with dreams of being a gunner on B-29s. Instead, after enlistment he was shuffled into Security Forces. He had hoped security would be a simple assignment, but it proved quite complicated and turned into an extended deployment to war.

During this time, the Air Force was experimenting with using a handful of sentry dogs (which some believed had been bred from dogs confiscated in Japan during World War II) to guard the wreckage of downed aircraft.[17] The parts left behind in wreckage were invaluable to both the Chinese and the Koreans: U.S. aviation secrets could be uncovered in those broken pieces, giving the desperate Koreans something of conceivable value to sell to Cold War communists on the black market.

Sentry dogs had proven they could guard in remote places, in extreme heat or cold, against the type of treachery and thievery the military was facing in Korea. The Air Force decided sentry dogs were their best chance at protecting invaluable assets, so they paired them with a very select contingent of security forces for this work. Airman O'Gara, seemingly by the luck of the draw, was one of the few men chosen to do the job. Not long after getting orders to Korea, O'Gara learned he would be meeting a new partner—a German Shepherd from Japan named Adwin.

During his first Korean winter in 1953, O'Gara became convinced that Korea was the coldest place on earth. The wind and blowing snow were almost unbearable for any living creature and, based on his earliest interactions with Adwin, O'Gara was sure he would receive no comfort from his dog, either: Adwin was one mean dog. The rumor floating around base was that Adwin had been a sentry dog for elite Japanese guards during World War II and was confiscated by the Americans during occupation. Regardless of where or how he learned to be mean, O'Gara had a terrible time "getting in on" Adwin, and it took a long time to convince him that they were going to be stuck together for the duration. Worse still, the other security police put O'Gara in a separate Kwanza Hut because, as they said, "Dog handlers have a constant stink." In every way, the young airman was truly out in the cold.

Luckily, Adwin had to have his can of frozen horsemeat thawed before he could eat. This meant that O'Gara had a pot belly stove for the task. Feeding time became their bonding time, a comforting ritual.

Adwin would wait out in his kennel for his meal, and Bob would soak up the warmth of the stove while preparing it. Man and dog, over time, came to rely on their partnership for survival and, maybe more importantly, for companionship. Ultimately Bob came to see the dog as more than a weapon; Adwin was a trusted partner and, in spite of his testy temperament, became his closest friend.

The long nights in frightful darkness and solitude tested the team's mettle. The night was full of danger, and Adwin was keenly aware of it all. He lived to protect O'Gara, who knew all too well what Adwin's alerts could be signaling. They fed off each other's energy, and often adrenaline would take over. Often they were called to crash sites where danger perpetually lurked in the shadows. O'Gara didn't want to release his dog on someone, but he was ready if necessary. He knew Adwin would do anything to protect him—even if it meant killing someone. Yet even more unbearable than the thought of having to kill someone (someone who might simply be trying to feed a family) were the actual crash sites themselves. The carnage and twisted bodies, the smell of burning fuel and flesh, the desolation, were often too much for man and dog to endure. O'Gara could only stroke his dog and speak reassuring words while Adwin whimpered softly in shared sadness.

The partners met every challenge together. But when O'Gara received orders home, he also received orders for Adwin to return to Japan. He realized that Adwin would never come back to the United States. The dog was too aggressive for most people, and even though O'Gara had learned to care for this military working dog, he wouldn't be given the option to take him home, either: the Air Force had invested a great deal of time and money in Adwin. He was a valuable asset, and they would not let him retire, even to the home of the man who understood him better than anyone else. Adwin would be passed on to a new handler to continue working. O'Gara was somewhat comforted by that thought but knew that no one could ever know Adwin the way he had.

After leaving Adwin, O'Gara's heart grew heavy. He missed his friend, the only other living soul who had witnessed the same visions of war and felt the same fear and despair. In spite of a nagging feeling that he should never look back, he asked the unit in Japan about Adwin. The reply came: Adwin had been euthanized by electrocution because he was too aggressive to be handled.

Bob O'Gara grieved for Adwin for the rest of his life. He wished he could have at least put the dog down himself, sparing his friend that cruel death. He would have shot him quickly, and with the greatest love and respect. O'Gara only hoped the world would remember the dog's incredible sacrifice; he was never able to forget.

2

HARLAN

In the spring of 1933, Harlan Hoffbeck was born to one of three Danish immigrant families inhabiting a small slice of the Three Lakes Township of Morgan, Minnesota. The Great Depression had hit their farming community hard. Their only hope of a continued existence was their little piece of land and the animals inhabiting it. The members of Harlan's family were intimately intertwined with the cycle of life, and they understood, in a way only farming folk can, what animals mean for survival.

The livestock on the Hoffbeck farm received the best care before being taken to market, and all other animals were there to support that end. The Hoffbecks had a horse team to pull a wagon or a plow, and there were dogs to protect the more valuable animals. Harlan learned early on to appreciate the valuable job dogs performed on a

farm. Only occasionally in his boyhood did he enjoy the companionship a dog can offer.

When Harlan was a baby the family lived in the granary on his
paternal grandfather's farm. His grandfather had built the entire farm
with his hands, including buildings, fences, and home. There were no
luxuries there—no plumbing, no electricity, no proximity to other
people—but there was the definite possibility of scratching out a life
in that place. Yet the Depression worked against them, and the family lost the farm at auction in 1938.

Young Harlan, his older sister, his older brother (mentally disabled
and blind from birth), and his parents moved on from their ancestral
farm, but not far. For a year they lived on the modest Madson Farm,
not more than ten miles away—but for Harlan it seemed like a million. There was no decent heat there capable of thwarting Minnesota
winters, and Harlan and his brother often went to the neighboring
Ulencamp Farm to gather the corn cobs out of their pigpen for burning in their little fireplace. One of Harlan's few memories of their
temporary home also came from the poverty that plagued the family.
His dad had bought two new tires on credit from Montgomery Ward,
and like many others in that time and place, he could not repay the
debt. When two strange men came down the farm road one day,
Harlan and his sister were each given a tire and told to hide in the
cornfield until the men left.

In 1939, the Hoffbeck family moved again to another home with
accommodations that were possibly the poorest of all. The Miller
Farm sat on a small, windy hill, and its buildings were no match for
the bitter cold. There was no electricity, no plumbing, and no phone.
The kitchen did have a pitcher pump, and they were forced to let the
prime go in winter, in order to keep it from freezing. Years of neglect
had left gaping holes in the walls and windows, which offered no

resistance to the howling winds and blowing northern snows. The three Hoffbeck kids shared an upstairs bed to keep warm. Their mother would nightly heat up irons, wrap them in towels, and put them at the foot of the bed to at least warm their frigid feet. Once the kids woke up to two inches of blown snow accumulated on their bedcovers.

In spite of its flaws, the Miller Farm was a home when many others had none. Harlan liked that the house was close to his school, only half a mile away. That little schoolhouse, Harlan's oasis, was one simple room, but built with sturdy walls. It had a great stove that adequately warmed eight students: three Larsons, two Druschs, three Hoffbecks, and their teacher, Ms. Ruth Hanson. Harlan always got to school before his teacher and would stare out the window, looking for the signal of her arrival: her Model-A Ford kicking up dust on the road. This meant the wood stove would soon be lit and the thought of that excited Harlan. First thing, Ms. Hanson would fling open the schoolhouse windows, telling the awaiting Hoffbeck kids, "Fresh air lights faster than stale." Harlan didn't mind being cold for a little longer. In the long run it was definitely warmer than home.

Just before World War II, the family moved to a better situation, a modest but comfortable two story house and barn on Judge Warren's farm. The judge paid Harlan and his sister fifty cents a day to pull mustard plants out of the oats, giving the children a way to help support the family. It was here that the family had their first telephone. And it was in this place that Harlan first became aware of the harsh reality of the value of animals on a farm. His father had always shielded him and his siblings from seeing the animals killed or butchered. But one day his father's march to the chicken coop sparked Harlan's natural boyish curiosity, and he peeked around the judge's barn door to find his dad ringing a chicken's neck. He was horrified—but wiser. Now he truly understood that animals were part of the family's survival.

There were other moves before Harlan ever went to high school, but the family's situation gradually improved. His mom found work at a bakery and his dad took up a cream route. The hours Harlan shared with his father were long and surprisingly hazardous. Farm dogs trained to protect property were never happy to see the Hoffbecks' truck lumbering down the lane. As far as these farm guardians knew, their cream was being stolen. Harlan learned a healthy dose of respect for dogs in these outings. He helped his dad with the route for a while, but after being run down and snapped at by too many disgruntled hounds, he decided to find another job. The bowling alley paid ten cents a game to set pins, and that was fine by Harlan. It was an occupation far less dangerous than outrunning testy guard dogs.

Harlan was still a young man when the war came to America on Pearl Harbor Day. By then his family had managed, like many other Minnesotans, to pull themselves out of the Depression's ruinous hole. They still weren't wealthy by any stretch, and it required the help of every able-bodied family member to contribute to the family income, especially with a nationwide war effort. Harlan thought of the soldiers serving overseas often, but unlike many boys in his grade, he didn't necessarily aspire to be like them someday. He had hopes of college and a job which would take him away from the hard-scrabble life of farming.

Post-war, Harlan's family had a home in town, next to his grandparents, and many comforts they had never enjoyed before. Harlan had kept his job at the bowling alley and had picked up a few other odd jobs as well throughout high school. It had been difficult to save, but where there was a will…and by his senior year, he had managed the grades, and the nest-egg, to buy at least a semester of college.

Harlan was smart, but he found college to be a challenge. It was difficult to keep up with classes, work, and family responsibilities. After his first semester, Harlan reluctantly accepted his failure. Still, going home without a promising income was not an option. He needed to find a fresh start with some hope of independence. Many of his friends had found that in military service, and Harlan decided the Army was as good a place as any to look. With some hesitation, he volunteered for the draft. On January 29, 1953, he was officially drafted into service in the U.S. Army, board number one hundred. The Korean War was still raging.

Harlan was sent from his little hometown, Morgan, Minnesota, to Fort Ord, California, for basic training. Because he had a little more life experience than most of the other guys in basic, with a whole semester of college under his belt, the training instructors gave him more responsibility. They saw him as a natural leader. Harlan breezed through basic because his adaptation to military life was not that big a transition. He had known struggle in a personal way, even as a little boy, living through bitter cold and hunger. Basic was, more or less, a breeze.

The only thing hanging over Harlan's head was the shot line—a whole line up of immunizations given in rapid succession. Not that Harlan feared shots, but there were so many of them. These were not just the basic inoculations for new soldiers either. As Harlan saw his shot record filling up with mark after mark, he realized that many of the diseases he was being vaccinated against had been nearly eradicated in America or had never developed here at all. The U.S. Army was preparing their new recruits for an exotic deployment. He knew right away he was bound for Korea.

Passing through the headquarters building one afternoon, Harlan noticed a sign on the bulletin board.

"Join the Doggies!"

"Trainers and handlers needed!"

"Sign up today."

Harlan knew that K-9 training could take as long as six months to complete. At least six months deferment before going to Korea? Without hesitation, he picked up the little pencil dangling from the bulletin board by a piece of yarn and signed his name. Surely the conflict would be over within six months. Of course, there was no guarantee he would be picked, but he hoped they would remember the leadership he had displayed in basic and would call his name for this selective duty. He feared that his life depended on it. When Harlan received word that he had been selected, he felt a combination of relief and trepidation. Harlan was glad that he might avoid Infantry duty on the now infamous front lines of Korea, but he really wasn't as knowledgeable about dogs as it might seem; he hoped he hadn't bitten off more than he could chew. This was going to be a shell game, but one that he hoped he could pull off.

GRETA

Harlan had never been a dog lover, but he respected the power and aggression of a dog—maybe more than most, given his experiences riding the family cream truck back home. As his bus pulled up to his new home at Camp Carson in the late spring of 1953, Harlan felt some trepidation. The sign out front reading 8125th Sentry Dog Detachment only made the butterflies in his stomach flutter harder.

The day after their arrival, the men were taken to the kennels where they would meet their dogs for the first time. Their arrival was surprisingly unceremonious. The sergeant handed Harlan his dog's paperwork. He had been given the only spayed female certified German Shepherd in the group. She had been shipped from the kennel where she was born in Silver Springs, Maryland, to Falls Church, Virginia. There, she received her vaccinations (probably not as many as Harlan), but very little else. In an odd shift from World War II policy, the dogs which came to the 8125th, at least initially, were not tattooed with a serial number. Without the serial number, the dogs could not be easily identified as military equipment. No one knows if military officials planned to send the dogs back to former owners at the end of this trial run, and therefore did not identify the dogs as their own. Perhaps it was an oversight or something miscommunicated as a task to be done before shipping her off to her next active assignment. Either way, Greta had been ushered into camp, it seemed, as an after-thought.

As the men entered the kennels for the first time, the sergeant warned them: "Some of the dogs are mean, some aren't. You're gonna have to be smarter than the dog, and just a heads-up—some of you aren't going to make it."

As Harlan walked down the rows of dogs, he felt a little smaller than his actual six-foot height. Dogs snarled, snapped, and showed teeth as he slinked by their individual kennels. He was thankful for the chains that held them in place. Some dogs were indifferent to the presence of a stranger, just as the sergeant had said. Many even seemed happy as their tails wagged and tongues lolled. Harlan looked at every kennel, searching for her name. Suddenly, he found it. Her placard read simply, Greta. Thoughts of the farm came rushing back to him, and he knew it was time to put his fears aside and get to work.

Harlan sat next to his beautiful Shepherd and slowly reached inside her kennel. Greta, aware of his presence but suspicious, shifted her butt to his approach and lay down with a sigh. She was tense, a

70-pound, muscular beast, uncertain about what this stranger wanted from her. Harlan understood that for both their sakes he had to move slowly. The trust they would build in those first few days was critical.

"Hey girl," Harlan softly chanted, reaching to scratch her around the tail. Greta shifted, softened just a little, and adjusted. Harlan lost track of how long he sat there before going to get her food. For two days this ritual continued before Harlan got the courage, and before Greta willingly submitted, to slip the choke chain around her neck, signifying they were ready to be partners.

Their first preparation for war came in the form of obedience training. Much to his surprise, Harlan found Greta was already an expert on obedience. It seemed as if she knew this stuff by heart, and the training was more for his benefit than hers. She could follow a limitless amount of commands. The "sits," "downs," and "stays" were seamless. For the first time in his life, Harlan was impressed by what a dog could actually do—besides chasing cream collectors. It was apparent to him that she had seen this type of training before. Greta respected Harlan, hanging on his every word, waiting for a motion of his arm or a flick of his wrist to fly into action. She still had to put him in his place from time to time, often cocking her head to the side, looking at him like she thought him stupid.

All in all, Harlan's time in training was going better than even he had imagined. Although he missed his mom, he had adequate downtime to write to her often. He wondered how to tell her that this was better than he had imagined, and even the Korean War, looming over everyone's head, was not as terrifying as it first seemed, especially with a dog by his side. Word at Camp Carson was that some resolutions were being reached in Korea and our nation's involvement there wouldn't last very long. Regardless, he could rely on Greta. He trusted her to be his lifeline in even the worst of times. In July 1953, before any deployment orders came, Harlan wrote home to ease his mother's mind.

July, 1953

Hi,

Was very glad to get your letter and should have answered earlier but the nights go by to [sic] fast. I really like it here. Some things are boring but with the food and good offices you can't get disgusted. My dog is really smart. Sure hope I can keep her. She sits, heels, stops, comes, and lays [sic] down when I give her the commands. I'm going to take a picture of her this afternoon which I will send home as soon as it gets back. I'm on a detail this week to water and feed the dogs and then next weekend I'll have off. It's really been hot down here lately but accord [sic] to the paper it's about same back home. My dog hasn't eaten for the last three days but I think it's because of the heat and then it drinks to [sic] much water just like a person does. We only feed them once a day and that's about 4:00 o'clock [sic] in the afternoon. Then we clean and water them and get back to the barracks at 5, eat supper and get a pass if we want. We get up at 5 in the morning which isn't bad at all. The food is really delicious and they always give you enough. One morning we had two eggs, bacon, hot cakes, cereal, and toast plus milk, butter and coffee. I think that's pretty good.

The men of the 8125th took meticulous care of their dogs. Grooming was thorough, and all dogs were regularly vet-checked to make sure that they were well and able to work. In turn, the dogs lived for their handlers. It seemed to the men that the more they cared for the dogs' basic needs, the more the dogs poured out their undying love and devotion. They would jump for joy at the very sight of their handlers and relished the new jobs they had been given. Greta too, in spite of a temporary loss of appetite in her early training (Harlan thought most likely due to her excessive water consumption after a stressful shipment to Carson), remained healthy under Harlan's doting care. She and Harlan were forming an incredible bond, and she was delighted to see him walking to the kennels every day.

Soon, Greta and Harlan were given the green light to start their aggression training. Harlan was uncertain about how it would go. The night before their new training regimen began, he brushed Greta and fitted her with a new leather collar. From that day forward the leather collar, different from the choke chain used in obedience, would be a signal to Greta that it was time to work. Just the simple act of putting the collar on made her haunches stiffen and caused her to

Agility training. The dogs were always rewarded for "bad behavior."

stand a little taller than before. Harlan wondered if she knew what they were going to undertake, both in training and in war. He wondered if her aggressive behavior would grow through training—and he both hoped and feared that it would.

HARLAN AND GRETA

In aggression training, Harlan found out what the sergeant meant when he warned that some dogs were already aggressive. Apparently, some of the unit's dogs had been sold to the Army precisely because they were ferocious.

Harlan, however, had to do the required work of consistent aggression training with Greta after she tested for scouts or sentries. She had gone through a dark house and alerted to a hidden "assailant" by barking. A bark, whether aggressive in nature or not, automatically meant that a dog was destined for sentry work. So Greta and Harlan, partnered for the duration, went to sentries. It didn't matter to Greta. She was there to please Harlan, and Harlan took some comfort in knowing she would remain his loyal protector.

Harlan noted the difference between Greta and other naturally aggressive dogs in the program. Private Jensen's dog, King, was one of the most ferocious dogs any of the men had ever seen. King attacked his handler more than once, one time breaking his collar and turning to lunge, leaving Jensen bloodied. The protocol of praise and never punish left Jensen no choice but to pat King after the incident and tell him, "Good boy!"

When graduation day came, Harlan and Greta were as ready as they could be. The team graduated with honors. Seventy-five young men, and over a hundred eager dogs, were ready to deploy together. Harlan knew Greta was a great dog and that she would protect him with her life. Their orders clearly put them in the direction of war, leaving out of Seattle aboard the USS *Howze*, with only one possible destination: Korea.

Their entire training process together had taken only ten short weeks.

KOREA

The USS *Howze* had served as a Navy transport vessel in the Pacific during the height of World War II, commanded by U.S. Coast Guard Captain Lee Baker. The ship was decommissioned in 1946 and handed over to the U.S. Army Department of Transportation. The Military Sea Transportation Service acquired the vessel in 1950, and until late fall 1953 it served to ferry service members to Korea.[1] By the time the 8125th got to the *Howze*, the ship was close to the end of its life. Having a group of smelly dogs aboard would be of little consequence. Looking at the ship, Harlan wondered if it would hold up.

The dogs were loaded in their kennels by crane and sling. As the handlers boarded, it was their responsibility to take the kennels—two men at a time carrying their dog-laden parcels—to the hull of the ship where the dogs would stay for the duration. The handlers saw this as the perfect opportunity to smuggle booze and loaded each of the kennels up with as much liquor as was comfortable for the dogs who shared the space. There wasn't much room for walking, watering, and feeding down in the hull, but the guys would have to make do; a bunch of rowdy Marines (who had boarded by climbing ropes up the side of the ship) were making the trip with them. Harlan noted that the ship's captain was not too thrilled with the Marines, but he was even less excited about the dogs. He could be heard wandering around the ship, mumbling under his breath, "Those damn dogs." Still, his disdain was not so great that he lacked compassion. The 8125th lost a dog while at sea, and the captain arranged for the military working dog to receive the full honors, due to any military member, and to give him a proper burial at sea.

It took thirty days to get to Japan, where the Marines were unloaded. The men of the 8125th got to walk around on the dock while the Marines disembarked. The dogs, however, never left the ship until their final destination. In the end they spent a month and a half aboard ship, before reaching Incheon Landing.

They could smell the stench of Korea for at least a mile out. It was so offensive a smell that even men and dogs who had been in cramped quarters for nearly two months recoiled. The dogs whimpered in their crates as they got closer to land, their hackles bristling with nervous energy. Many of the handlers wondered if the dogs could smell their digested canine cousins oozing out of the pores of the starving Korean people. Greta seemed to be imploring Harlan to help her escape from that place.

From Incheon, it would be a day's drive to their new home. The sentry dogs, still in their kennels, were loaded onto the backs of trucks headed for Yong Dong Po, Ascom City, Korea. The contingent of scout dogs which came over with them went to an unknown destination. Their paths would not cross again.

The sentry dogs settled in to their new homes with ease, while their handlers committed to keeping them on a regular schedule. There was plenty of work to be done already built into their day. The 8125th had been tasked on arrival with guarding an ammunition storage warehouse. The post was rife with pilfering by Korean civilians who were desperate for anything of value which could be sold to support starving families. And the Koreans were terrified of these particular dogs more than wild animals. Their ferocity was notorious and therefore one of the most valuable psychological weapons available. The Korean civilians often threw rocks at the dogs out of disdain. Harlan and the men allowed it, however, knowing that this would only make the dogs more aggressive to potential thieves. Dogs had proven, during World War II and after, to be the Army's best protection against loss. So the 8125th were welcomed and ready to achieve the mission set before them.

Though the war was arguably winding down in 1953, tensions remained. The North Koreans had held on with all their power and used every means to continue psychological warfare on American troops. Harlan took note of this tactic when he first arrived. Every evening for the first two months he was in Korea, "Bedcheck Charlie" paid a visit to their unit. This supposed North Korean, flying an open cockpit Piper Cub, would circle the camp dropping hand grenades as he went. At first the dogs barked and yelped, but it wasn't long before they realized this intruder was merely part of the landscape. By the time Bedcheck Charlie finally disappeared, the dogs no longer noticed.

Harlan and Greta spent almost all of their time together. All dog and handler teams worked two days on and one day off, twelve-hour shifts, 6:00 p.m. to 6:00 a.m. But outside of that, the handlers never went anywhere without their dogs. They went to the Post Exchange and chow with their dogs. They would socialize, limited as it was, with the dogs by their sides. Harlan and Greta only parted when he slept. She would go back to the kennel, a wooden dog house, where she was chained. The chain was long enough for Greta to get on top of the box or escape inside during inclement weather. Like the other dogs, Greta was never in her box for long. Greta was always happy to see Harlan when he returned and she would rise to meet him, excited to put on the leather collar signifying work was imminent.

The reality of the desperate situation for the Korean people soon became painfully apparent to the men tasked with guarding ammo.

Harlan found out early on that he and Greta weren't necessarily protecting valuable equipment from an organized military recon-force. Korean civilian employees were notorious on post for making themselves valuable and trusted workers so that they might gain entrance to the higher value equipment.

Once while Harlan and Greta were guarding the ammo dump, they experienced one of the most terrifying nights of their lives. The bombed-out ammo factory was creaky and creepy, making both Harlan and Greta's hair stand on end. This night they heard inexplicable rustling. Dog and man reverted to their training. Greta gave a hard alert to something under the floor. Harlan shouted a warning in English and Korean as Greta continued to bark and growl viciously. He debated releasing her, knowing that meant certain death for anybody under those floor boards. Holding her back, Harlan peeked under the floorboard and discovered an entire network of tunnels leading from the storm drainage system to the underbelly of the secured ammo storage site. Korean civilian contractors had mapped the site on their many visits, allowing them complete access to anything of value. "Papasan" would park the honey wagon outside the gate and await the pilfered treasure. Harlan was thankful there had not been a face on the other side of those boards; he and Greta had thwarted the barrage. They would encounter this same situation again and again for the rest of their days in Korea.

Harlan and the other men found it difficult to trust the Koreans, but at the same time they possessed great empathy for them. This was felt most keenly during the daily feeding of the dogs. The dogs received a daily ration of horse meat and Wheaties, which the Army supplied in plentiful amounts. The men were under orders to dispose of the many expired cans of leftover meat. The Koreans knew when the food was disposed of because civilian employees would spread the word to their families outside the gate. It wasn't uncommon to see Korean men, women, and children rushing to the trash truck as it made its way outside. In desperation they would hang off the truck's tailgate, hoping to get a scrap from the heap of discarded horse meat. For some of the soldiers, this was the first time they had seen starvation with their own eyes. For Harlan, it reminded him of the hunger he and his family had known back in Minnesota. It was a nearly insurmountable task to meet the needs of so many, and Harlan was never as pained by turning them away as some of his fellow soldiers were.

He wasn't, however, lacking in compassion. In general, Harlan carried out his duties with a mutual understanding for the needy people of Korea. He tried to help whenever feasible, just like neighbors helped neighbors back home. Some ways of aiding the needy were more palatable to him than others. He loved playing Santa Clause for the local children at Christmastime. Although he wasn't as portly as St. Nick, Harlan was tall and all-around big. This translated well to Korean children who had learned about Santa through missionaries and soldiers and had bought into the lore of an elf who was bigger than life. Giving gifts to the children gave Harlan joy when he was so far from home.

In another empathetic gesture, the men would often take a Korean child under their wing and try to help them, to the best of their ability. Harlan and his tent-mates took in a young Korean as a houseboy. The boy did light chores, laundry, and sweeping. In return, the men would give the boy food for himself and his family. Sometimes they offered money, or even items to be sold by the boy's family, but these were of little importance to them. Their immediate need rose from hunger.

It wasn't just the humans outside the camp who were desperate for nourishment. The scent of horse-meat being warmed on potbelly stoves for the K-9s also brought in the area's starving dogs. These strays found respite there. American soldiers viewed dogs as pets or working animals, but never food. Both figuratively and literally, strays found sanctuary with the 8125th and often became part of their family. The male sentry dogs were rarely neutered and puppies were born from the union of strays and military working dogs. Those puppies, more often than not, found their way into the tents and hearts of American servicemen.

Harlan's tent had taken in one such stray puppy, and their houseboy seemed to enjoy playing with it. The men could also be found offering shoelaces to chase and things for the puppy to chew. There was always more than enough horse meat for the working dogs, so at the end of their shifts they would bring some back to feed the puppy. It didn't take long for the tent's mascot to become roly-poly.

The houseboy, who was the puppy's playmate while the men were working, one day asked if he could keep the puppy for himself. The men all agreed that it seemed like a natural fit, so they gave their mascot away. The next day when their houseboy returned for his regular duties, the men asked how the puppy had done his first night in a new home.

"He was very good," the boy reported matter-of-factly. "My family ate him right away. They are very grateful." Many of the men were sickened and to the boy's chagrin, visibly disturbed.

Harlan, who understood hunger in an intimate way, shrugged. "You can't fault the boy for taking care of his family."

Throughout the sixteen months that this first wave of the 8125th were in Korea, the job remained constant—and the pressures remained as well. The men would do just about anything to blow off steam. With plenty of money on hand and lots of free time, they drank away the hours playing cards and carousing with the local girls. Once, the guys thought it would be funny to invite the straight-laced officers to one of their raucous parties. The doctor, the local missionary, and the chaplain all made the guest list. The men giggled at the thought of making these puritans blush—that is, if they had the audacity to show up. But when the night came around and all three attended, the party fell into an awkward lull. Then the chaplain ordered a round of drinks for their little group of good guys.

"Well, hell," Harlan told the others. "Looks like we're not the only ones who need to forget this place for a while." The evening then went off without a hitch as the guys shared in their misery and celebration.

Harlan had an obligation to send money home and always tried to keep an eye on what he was spending. He had set up an allotment of almost half his pay to go home, or so he thought, but because of a clerical error, what he believed was $40 per month was actually $80. This left him with about $10 to burn (not counting the extra money earned from selling cigarettes) on poker. He relied heavily on his buddy Hiller, one of six fellow Minnesota boys who had come to Ascom City with Harlan, to be his banker. Sometimes, Harlan and Hiller would clean up and Hiller would keep him in check. Most times it was a wash.

Booze was the only escape for many of the guys, and sometimes a GI would get out of control. At least once a month, someone would inevitably pass out drunk while on duty. In this situation, being a dog handler had its advantages. The guys had learned how to use their dogs to protect them in all situations. Steark from Washington was notorious for passing out drunk with his dog lashed to his arm for protection. Once on second shift he stopped by the club for a few beers and promptly passed out in the street. The Sergeant of the Guard walked by and tried to grab Steark's carbine—the protocol for proving dereliction of duty. His dog, trained to protect his handler from any threat, lashed out at this would-be assailant. There was no getting around the keen attention of the military working dog. In the end, Steark was left to sleep it off while his dog rested by his side, confident that he had fulfilled his duties.

LEAVING

Harlan had never been particularly fond of dogs. Ironically, he had only joined the Doggies as a way of avoiding duty in Korea. Yet now he had such an abiding respect and admiration for Greta. Her strength, power, and devotion were unlike anything he had ever experienced before. And above all else, Greta was loyal.

One time there was a dog loose in the kennel. Harlan had stumbled in not knowing the dog was free. When he figured it out, panic set in. He was familiar with the loose dog, but he was not that dog's person—it had no loyalty to him whatsoever. He had played agitator so many times that in this instance that instinct had kicked in, and he froze in place. The snarl and icy stare of the loose dog remained. The only one who could protect him was bound up in her own kennel, unable to come to his side. Reacting from his gut, he called to Greta in her kennel. Greta, living to please him, returned with a familiar yip. Something in Greta's recognition—a kind of primal recognition in the dog's language—distracted the loose dog. His hackles went down and he unlocked his attention from Harlan. Harlan went to Greta and thanked her. She had been his lifeline all along. As Harlan's time drew to a close, he was surprised to feel, in some ways, melancholy. For eighteen months they had talked about nothing else but getting home. They missed the food, their families, their beds. Many had girlfriends and wives waiting. Harlan had joined the Army hoping to stay out of Korea, and in predictable military fashion, Korea was exactly where he ended up. But for the men of the 8125th, going home proved bittersweet. Half of the division would remain in Korea, awaiting new handlers. The men had bonded with their dogs and formed relationships, enjoying a closeness that even their human interactions lacked.

The day Harlan was to board his ship bound back to the states, he debated going to say good-bye to Greta. Not having her at his side in that moment felt so strange—she had been with him almost every minute for the past eighteen months. He decided not to go to her kennel. It would only be confusing, not only for him but for Greta. He knew that she would sense the good-bye from his posture and his emotion; even his smell would even betray what he felt. He thought about Greta's next handler, knowing that whoever he was, he would never share the same bond with Greta. He hoped he was a tough son-of-a-bitch, because Greta could be a handful.

Greta.

Harlan.

"That's one mean dog," Harlan laughed to himself.

He knew that her new handler had been trained to the same rigor. He took comfort in that. He said a silent farewell to Greta in his heart, grabbed his rucksack, and headed toward home, looking forward to the comforts that awaited him.

On returning home, Harlan found a world less welcoming than he had imagined. Signs in bar windows were foreboding. "No military in uniform allowed." The folks back home didn't want to talk about Korea. People were through with war.

Sometimes it felt like his time in Korea had all been a dream. If only he had Greta by his side, he would have known for sure it had been real. She had been his comfort and protection from a hostile world. Back in the states, he felt certain she would have been his shield from this apathetic one. Over time the reality set in that he would be better off forgetting his eighteen months in Korea. Greta, however, would never leave him. She remained a ghost, heeling at his side, from then on.

3

PRINZ

By the time Prinz arrived in the world, people had already formed ideas and had great expectations for him. He was not born to a run-of-the-mill backyard breeder but had been given all advantages from the beginning. He was born in a kennel of quality German Shepherds owned by prominent couple Howard and Doris Grafftee of Skowhegan, Maine. His sire had been one of twenty-two puppies from the direct line of notable AKC champion "Nox of Ruthland." Prinz and all his litter-mates had the finest pedigree and were from their whelping spoken for, anticipated, and loved.

The popularity of German Shepherds in the 1950s had grown exponentially from the decade before. Their reputation for strength, endurance, and loyalty, earned during their brave service in World War II, had forever endeared them to the American public. The show *Rin Tin Tin*—only one of the many incarnations of the famous military companion dog born on the battlefield in France during World War I—first aired in 1954 and was the pinnacle of popularity for the breed.[1]

By 1954 the German Shepherd had, by most accounts, become America's favorite dog breed. Breeders across the country, under AKC guidelines, produced quality stock. But German Shepherds were more than show dogs. Their multi-faceted character appealed to the military and police alike, so many backyard breeders cropped up to fill the demand. It was the German Shepherd's application as sentry, sentinel, sniffer, and security guard which created its most enduring purpose. No longer were Shepherds relegated to guarding livestock. Now they were recognized as guardians and fierce defenders of men. However, pairing soldiers and Shepherds had just as much to do with the dogs' companionship as their ferocity. Simply put, German Shepherds love their people. The hallmark of the breed is complete devotion, and they have earned the reputation of being "one-man dogs."[2]

In his first days, Prinz rooted in the darkness for the warmth of his mother's coat and the nourishment of her milk. His place in the pack was secure early on. He was sociable with his litter mates. The lovely black and tan markings across his muzzle made his newly opened eyes stand out. He was attentive and alert. The breeders admired his countenance and disposition, too, making him a favorite litter member.

As Prinz grew he remained one of the most beautiful pups in the bunch. Although he was not the very top pick in a litter full of fabulous specimens, he was very close. It would be hard to stand out in a group of dogs sired by a champion, but the minute details which may have been lacking in his physical appearance were made up for in his demeanor. As he began to get his wobbly puppy legs under control, the pack also began spending more time in the cold Maine woods.

They ventured out to pee on things, of course, but they also were being exposed to a whole new world of sounds, sights, and smells. Prinz's people watched him closely, knowing he had a home awaiting him where some dreams had already been built around the kind of dog he would become. They watched to see the way the little pup would react to new surroundings, and they were consistently pleased. Prinz was adventurous and bold. He had an incredible knack for scenting and was alert to his surroundings. Most of all, though, Prinz was lovingly attentive to people.

Gerry Ballanger was a teacher at a local community college and wasn't a wealthy man. He had loved dogs from childhood, and this love had led to aspirations of showing dogs on the AKC circuit. Showing at that level of prestige would be costly, but he believed the right dog would be a worthwhile investment. There were several breeds he had shown as an amateur, but German Shepherds intrigued him. He had never shown the breed before, but its beautiful lines, impeccable conformation, strength, and reputation for bravery appealed to him.

A friend of Gerry's, an ophthalmologist named Doctor Osler of Bangor, Maine, had connections to Prinz's kennel in Skowhegan and connected Gerry to the Grafftees. Doctor Osler had built up a reputable little kennel of his own. He involved his kids in the kennel operations, and they had spent plenty of family weekends at AKC dog shows. His son Jay enjoyed showing, especially the ribbons and trophies. Daughter Mary Jay was just a kid and didn't care much for that part of the kennel business, but she spent countless hours with the dogs handling and playing with the puppies. The puppies were her favorites. She gave them invaluable socialization, and Doctor Osler encouraged it. He would certainly rather his daughter chase puppies instead of boys.

Gerry let the Grafftees know he was looking for the best of the litter, but he couldn't necessarily afford the price tag associated with the top pick. The Grafftees had had their eye on Prinz from the beginning, knowing he could be a great dog in his own right, though he wasn't the pick of the litter. They came off the price a bit for Gerry and asked for $50. That was still an exorbitant amount for Gerry to pay for a dog. The first time he saw Prinz, however, he felt sure the regal pup could be the seed of something really good. His kennel would be born through Prinz.

During the eight-week waiting period after Prinz's birth, Gerry wondered about the puppy's personality. He wondered if he had made the right choice and if he could ever see a return in his $50 investment. Meanwhile, he picked a name for his kennels and the new pup: Ball-Moore Kennels would be the future home of Prinz Lamie von Shepwold. He thought the name sounded right. It was another step toward a thriving kennel operation.

Although Gerry and Doctor Osler had no shared financial interest in the kennel, Gerry valued the doctor's opinion and experience with the German Shepherd breed. The doctor offered his advice on making a champion whenever he could, and Gerry willingly took any suggestions. So when Mary Jay Osler found out that Gerry had a new puppy coming home, she promised her dad that she would do her part in making Prinz, "a great dog." Doctor Osler felt good about that arrangement.

On the day Gerry went to pick up Prinz, he was eager and excited. He hoped Prinz would be the dog he had imagined, but he also looked forward to the companionship a dog consistently gives. He felt a warm contentment at the thought of having Prinz by his side for the next ten to fifteen years—hopefully to the end of the dog's life expectancy.

Meanwhile, waiting in his kennel, Prinz sensed it was a different kind of day. He anxiously paced and hopped, tongue lolling out of his mouth, knowing instinctively that his person was coming. As dogs do, Prinz was living in the moment. The moment was good and worthy of his eager anticipation—enough for him.

The meeting was quick. Gerry came in, picked up Prinz's certification paperwork, slipped a new collar around his fluffy throat, and gave a curt, "Let's go boy!" He couldn't wait to get Prinz home and start getting to know him. Prinz jumped obediently into the back seat of the car knowing an adventure was afoot. "My person," was written all over his exuberant face. His eyes were fixed constantly on the man he already knew as his best friend.

In the days and weeks and months that followed, Prinz came to realize there were many people he could call "his." Of course, Gerry was his main person, but he came to know many more who offered treats, pats, and play. There was the girl, "Mary Jay," who rolled on the floor with him and scratched his belly. Prinz thought she was very nice, and he looked forward to her regular visits. Then there were all the little people at the place Gerry called "the school."[3] They were great fun for Prinz, and he counted his days with them as some of his very favorites. The little ones played and jumped over things and ran really fast, always with Prinz at their sides. Sometimes he would jump things, or go into tunnels, or just walk on a leash in a circle, and he would be rewarded for it all. They had two wheel devices that made the most curious noises as they whizzed around him. The kids offered him pats and treats, and they smelled great—all of a dog's favorite smells rolled into one fragrant bouquet.

As Prinz grew, so did his responsibilities to Gerry. He learned many things that were important to his person: "sit," "stay," "speak," "watch me," and "down." None of these were difficult to learn, and as long as he was by Gerry's side he didn't mind doing them. Man and dog traveled all over, performing these commands for other people. Usually Prinz got rewards for his work, and he thought that was nice.

After Prinz had seen one summer come and go, Gerry decided to let him smell another dog up close. Of course he had smelled other dogs before, but this time he got to smell the other dog off leash and without restraint. Her scent was pleasing to him and before he knew it, Prinz was being referred to as "sire."

Many of the puppies Prinz sired came and went. One of them captured Gerry's attention, however, and this one, named Pharaoh, stayed. Prinz liked Pharaoh. His company gave Prinz another dog with which to do dog things. The two went on to share many adventures. Prinz took on his fatherhood role with pride and shared Gerry with the younger dog, showing Pharaoh the joys of getting affection from a beloved handler. Prinz also taught the youngster his secrets of the trade, showing the pup the most important aspect of doghood: to guard and protect the most valuable asset they knew, their people.

Mary Jay still made her special visits, and now Pharaoh was included in their work.

"Watch him!" Mary Jay would tell Prinz, and he would lock onto his subject (usually Gerry) with a cold and unflinching gaze. Pharaoh absorbed his sire's behavior like a sponge and before long was locking on with the same sharpness. The pup possessed an equal wit to his sire. Both benefitted from generations of great breeding.

It was only natural for Prinz to be out of sorts when the pup eventually joined another pack.[4] Often Prinz roamed the house looking for his friend, making his call to him with no response. Gerry comforted him with the command, "Settle," and stroked his hand across Prinz's soft back. He would never see Pharaoh again, but he was comforted by Gerry's constant presence. Still, a sense of uneasy change charged the air in Ball-Moore kennels. Talk and tone among the people had changed, and Prinz perked his ears to take in the new vibrations.

DUTY CALLS

Gerry and Doctor Osler talked about the possibilities for hours. Bills were piling up, and Gerry simply could not make ends meet. He knew Prinz was the funnel through which the money left his pocket, and he also knew that it was no one's fault. He had given Prinz all he could for as long as possible, and the dog had given his all to him and then some. Now Gerry knew he had to find the best possible situation for his dog.

Perhaps Osler could take Prinz into his kennel and work him into his program? The doctor was reluctant. His was a hobby kennel, and the kids had begun to lose interest. Jay would be going to college soon and Mary Jay had her school and theater activities. They were just too busy for an active dog like Prinz. He needed an outlet for his superior intellect and could never be relegated to an occasionally attended pet. Mary Jay, holding back the tears, protested, "Daddy I can make time. He's such a good boy. I'll make time."

"Mary Jay, you're not being sensible. I promise you'll grow out of it, this dog phase, then there will be boys. No. We just can't take him on."

Gerry felt a tightening knot in his throat. He knew that Mary Jay loved Prinz, and if she only loved him with a fraction of what he felt for the dog, it would be enough. He wanted to cry, but he realized that this day had always been a possibility. He couldn't feel sorry for himself.

Dr. Osler suggested, "I read in the *Bangor Daily News* that the Army was looking for German Shepherds for their Military Working Dog Program. They're paying good money, Gerry. It could be a viable solution."

Gerry wondered if it could be a good solution. It was noble, for sure. And he knew that the dogs would not be isolated, left to rot in a kennel or tied out to a stake in someone's backyard. He rolled the thought around in his head, aching under the weight of knowing he would never see Prinz again if he gave him away. He asked, "Are the dogs cared for?"

"They are worked," Doctor Osler replied. "You remember the dogs during the war? They were heroes."

Gerry hesitated.

"They are offering $150.00 for dogs that fit their parameters, Gerry."

Days later, Gerry sent an inquiry to the U.S. Quartermaster. They were looking for German Shepherds of sound temperament, 25 to 28 inches in height, 75 to 90 pounds.[5] Prinz more than fit the bill. Gerry choked back the fear and told the clerk he had a possibility in Prinz. The Quartermaster's office put paperwork in the mail without hesitation and gave Gerry a date to expect the special crate for Prinz's delivery.

Although the war in Korea had slowed, it was still an excessively hostile place for American service members. Gerry briefly wondered, and even asked the quartermaster, about the possibility of Prinz being sent into the hostility in Asia. He was quickly reassured, "The sentry dogs are given the best and most rigid training in order to guard military installations. They are used largely in the European Command with several hundred already on duty at airfields, gasoline dumps, ammunition dumps, and supply depots, scattered from

Prinz sits for his formal portrait as a loved and prized show dog.

Prinz displays his sunny disposition.

Puppy Pharaoh and Proud Poppa Prinz regularly worked and played with children of all ages. Here they are a part of Gerry Ballanger's playground group in an amateur dog show.

Bremerhaven to Munich, from Berlin westward over the Army's line of communication through France and La Pallice on the Atlantic coast."[6] There was no guarantee in this statement, but Gerry felt the possibility of Prinz going to Korea was slim.

Prinz sniffed around the new wooden box when it arrived. It smelled of the trees in the woods of Maine but also something foreign and strange. He stepped inside and the low tones of wood rubbing against wood piqued his interest. He looked at the contraption, head cocked to one side then the other and wondered what he was meant to do as Gerry encouraged him forward. He sensed the same strange feelings of excitement he had known the day Gerry picked him up as a puppy, but he also felt the same sensations as the day Pharaoh left. The sadness pouring out of him made Prinz pause; he smelled different. Prinz licked his mouth, the deepest form of pack recognition, and stepped inside the box, spinning and pawing before finally settling in a furry ball. He looked at Gerry again for his next command.

"Good boy, Prinz," was all that Gerry could muster.

On Wednesday, November 18, 1953, Prinz became a soldier. He left via the Railway Express Agency, Union Station, Bangor, Maine, as many thousands of soldiers before him had done. He felt nervous, as evidenced by the pert ears and low growling ruff, and he also felt a deep pang of separation. Low tones turned to high yipping calls as he watched Gerry leave from between the slates of his crate. He didn't know if he would ever see him again.

His train whisked him down the East Coast to Cameron Station, Virginia, in a matter of hours. Once there, he received the same military physical that GIs have endured since forever: height, weight, shots, haircut, serial number (tattooed on the left flank). Once he was stamped "Qualified for Duty," his induction was official. He would be held in that crate, with occasional exercise, for the next twenty-one days.

The next stop after quarantine: Camp Carson, Colorado.

4

THE CALL

In 1946, Fort Ord, California, had taken on a new post-war significance for the United States Army. The post, which sprawled a lengthy distance along the Monterey Bay Peninsula, had been built up during World War II by prisoners of war taken following the D-Day invasion. They had been housed there during the remainder of the war and tasked with making it into a state-of-the-art training facility. That same year, Fort Ord became a basic military training post and advanced infantry training center. The Fourth Infantry Division called the post home for the next four years until being moved to Fort Benning in 1950, and then was replaced at Fort Ord by the 6th Infantry Division that same year. The Sixth then took on the main responsibility of readying soldiers for the Korean Conflict.[1]

In 1953, the Department of the Army started pulling soldiers from the infantry pool at Fort Ord to man a new unit. The 8125th Sentry

Dog Detachment was experimental at best. Hoping to build on the successes of the military working dog program in World War II, they concocted a security detail program consisting of farm boys from around the country and German Shepherds bought from civilians. Military officials believed farm boys could remain detached from the dogs because they were accustomed to using animals as tools to complete a job. The dogs were "issued equipment" and this select group of men, they believed, would use them as such. Their training regimen would be rigorous but worthwhile. The potential for saving the Army millions of dollars, by thwarting rampant thievery and pillaging, as well as the loss of U.S. military secrets by hostile spies, was foremost in their rationale.

RECRUITS

FICKES

At seventeen, John Robert Fickes was eager to see the world. His small Nebraska hometown—population 1,725 according to the 1940 census—offered little variety. His school—not his class but his school—had a total of eight students. He had seen the limits of Kimball, Nebraska, and then some.

When he traveled to the big city of Denver, Colorado, in 1952, the war raging in Korea never entered his mind. He walked into the recruitment office of the Air National Guard with the fresh face that is every recruiter's dream and announced, "I want an adventure."

The recruiter easily signed him into a seven-year contract with the Wyoming Air National Guard, and he left as fast as the bus would take him. Three months in, Fickes realized the Guard wasn't as exciting as he had thought it might be. On reflection, he realized his little hometown rearing had been a somewhat charmed existence. The comforts of community were great, and Kimball offered many things a boy wants. Just outside of town, Fickes's uncle owned a ranch a few hundred acres deep. He had enjoyed the farming well enough, but his favorite ranch activity was running the ranch horses with the farm dogs, a pack of coursing greyhounds. Sometimes they would hunt for coyotes, dogs swiftly skimming the earth and horses beating a thunderous drum as they ripped the ground beneath their steady hooves. But just as fun were the days when they would ride the ranch perimeter surveying fences, the dogs trotting alongside. The dogs were always a part of it, not just the greyhounds but retrievers for birds, Shepherds for livestock, and the occasional mutt for companionship. Fickes realized he had known a freedom that transcended Kimball's limits, and his canine friends had been a part of that liberation.

The Wyoming Air National Guard wasn't for him. In 1953 he went back to the recruiters pool in Denver, and this time he walked into the Army office. The Army recruiter made all the arrangements and secured him an Honorable Discharge from the Air Guard, signed him into the Army, and within a matter of weeks, put him on a bus to Basic Training at Fort Ord, California.

BROADWAY

That same year, a man in Jacksonville, Texas, was drafted into the Army at the age of nineteen. Despite being from a small town, Charles Broadway never felt the cozy familiarity of that life. He never even felt a closeness with his parents, brother, or two sisters. His dad fought hard to provide for the family as a carpenter, while everyone worked to keep their Texas farm going. Life was hard. The family's horses and dogs were essential for work, but Broadway never saw them as just tools. He relished their company, and the bird dogs were some of his favorites. Even though they were used to provide food for the family, he shared a special bond with them. The hours spent in their company, flushing grouse across the rolling bluebonnet-covered hills, were some of his favorite boyhood times.

Broadway's family couldn't afford to send him to college, but they had managed to save enough to send him to a trade school. He worked construction for a while fresh out of high school, but he believed he would soon be drafted. In December 1952, Broadway managed to secure a part-time job pouring concrete at Barksdale Air Force Base in Louisiana. A few months into his new job, he decided to take some time off around Christmas and return home. He had no money for travel, so he hitchhiked the 150 miles back. When he returned, there was a draft notice on the mantle waiting for him: he was to report for Army Basic Training on January 4.

Broadway completed basic training in El Paso, Texas, and was shuttled into an infantry slot right out of the gate. Advanced infantry training took place at Fort Ord, and an assignment there meant the certainty of being sent to the war in Korea. Broadway looked around and thought, "I don't wanna go with this bunch of guys who will certainly get us killed."

Apathy and reluctance to fight were the hallmark of his unit, predominantly made up of draftees. He prepared himself for the inevitable. So when orders came down for infantrymen to ship to Korea, he was elated and highly confused to find his name wasn't on the list.

"Airborne then," he thought, pondering the horrors of jumping out of a perfectly good airplane. Then he noticed that there were about fifteen others from his company who weren't on the orders either.

HATCH

In Utah, Grant Hatch lived a pastoral life in a small Mormon town. His family was big, and they were a tightly knit unit. Service was highly valued in their small farming community, and he felt that it would define his life. So when he and his two best friends, at the age of eighteen, went to join up for military service, they were following a community precedent. Many in their little town had gone before them.

They walked into the Naval recruiter hoping for jobs that would keep them together in the Buddy System.[2] Ultimately, Hatch didn't meet the Navy's qualifications, but his friends did. The Army was not as choosy, as soldiers were desperately needed on the ground in Korea. The Army took Hatch, while his two friends, at least initially, stayed together but went in a different direction than Hatch. In a matter of days Hatch was shipped off to Fort Ord for basic training.

FALGE

Bob Falge enjoyed a beautiful life in Willitts, California. The mighty redwoods towered just west of his little hamlet, and the mountains rose all around. The town itself was dotted with vast ranch lands of the old California tradition. The people foraged cattle there and had a deep and abiding tradition of horsemanship. Falge's family didn't personally own a large plot of land, but the ranches which encompassed their little home were just as much his domain. He had a horse and would ride out to neighboring ranches as often as he could. When he was sixteen, he tacked up his horse and rode to one of the ranches, taking his first legitimate job as a ranch hand. His job was checking and repairing fences, which he undertook daily with the companionship of his most trusted mare. Often the ranch dogs would come along as well. He thought his life was as pretty close to perfect, in those precious moments, as was humanly possible. Yet it was a life that he knew couldn't go on forever.

In 1953, at the age of eighteen, Falge volunteered for the draft. He went into the Army with no idea of where he would go or what he would do. The rhythm of ranch life had taught him to let the daily details take care of themselves. He was sent to Fort Ord for basic training, and he knew that each of the three possible positions he would likely fill after graduation could send him to Korea. When Falge finally received his orders, he was pleasantly surprised. The job lent itself well to his past experiences.

RATH

Eugene Rath, "Eddie" to his friends, grew up in a small, rural town in Laurel, Nebraska, with plenty of exposure to farm life. Having hunted with, explored with, and generally roamed with dogs his entire childhood, Rath figured dogs were pretty much one of God's best creations. He saw them as a benefit of small town life.

In 1952, talk around Laurel centered on the looming draft. At the age of eighteen, Rath understood there was no way to avoid it. He volunteered for Army service and by 1953 was enlisted. Sent to Fort Ord for basic training, he had no idea where the Army would take him, but he did know it would be an adventure. He was excited and proud to be serving his country. Even with all the hassle the Army can be, he felt that he was doing something worthwhile, and he was pleased.

BAKKEN

Orion Bakken was an ordinary farm kid from Milan, Minnesota. His family of two sisters and a brother lived a simple life on a farm, raising grain and cattle. Orion, "Ollie" as the other kids called him, was quiet but likable. There was a twinkle in his eye which gave away his underlying enthusiasm, but he could be content in solitude for hours. Many times, those hours were spent with the family dog.

Bakken grew into young adulthood and enlisted in the Army at the age of eighteen. He felt it was just a natural step to take and the right thing to do. His enlistment was a cut-and-dried, three-year commitment. He didn't know what the Army had in store for him and accepted his orders to Fort Ord without question.

PETERSON

Curtis Peterson also grew up in Milan, Minnesota. He and Bakken had known each other as kids. They lost track of one another when Peterson left school in the ninth grade, to work on the family farm. He joined the National Guard at the age of seventeen, but quit at eighteen to go active duty in the Army with two of his buddies. On January 4, 1954, Curtis went to Fort Riley, Kansas, for basic training. After graduation he went on to Fort Ord for infantry school. His orders to Camp Carson came as a surprise, but an even bigger surprise was being reunited with his old friend Orion Bakken.

STAHLKE

Larry Gean Stahlke was an independent Midwestern boy. One of four kids growing up on the family farm, he had a lot of responsibilities beyond school. Taking care of siblings and taking care of livestock was grueling work. He never much cared for being told what to do and was looking for an escape from his rigorous life. When he was seventeen, in an ironic twist for a rebellious spirit who hated the voice of authority, he talked his mom into signing him into the Army early. Somehow Stahlke knew that the Army would help him to grow up and become his own man—even though it would mean following orders more than ever before in his life.

JELLISON

Paul Raymond Jellison was a soft-spoken young man from rural Johnson, Kansas. His daddy was a pastor who believed in hard work and sent Raymond out to work on local farms. Raymond's natural next step in a servant's life was to enlist and do his part. Before leaving for Army duty, he married his high school sweetheart, Eva.

STEWART

Donald David Stewart was the youngest of five kids growing up on a family farm. The farm was inhabited with livestock, which included dogs. Stewart's father had instilled in him that dogs were always a farmer's tool and never a pet. One dog, Stewart later remembered, was used for herding cattle into the milking stalls. He really liked that dog, but his father didn't care for all of its behaviors. After the dog killed and devoured a dozen of the family's chickens, his father grabbed it and dragged it behind the barn in a fit of rage. Stewart cried and begged his father not to do it, saying, "I can train him to stop!" His father shot and killed the dog in front of him, reinforcing the idea in his young mind that dogs were only good as long as they were useful.

When Stewart was old enough, he went to Fort Riley, Kansas, and volunteered for the draft. He went into Basic Training at Fort Ord, knowing that he was destined for Army Infantry. When he was pulled from infantry with special orders, he never really questioned it. He thought it must be a fortunate turn of events in his favor, and he hoped it meant he could avoid the action in Korea.

BENEVENGA

Norlin J. Benevenga ("Ben") moved from the big city of San Francisco to the less populated part of Marin County, California, when he was a boy. His new home stood in stark contrast to where he had come from: the area only had fifty residents in total. The dairy farm, a few miles down the road, had other people and animals that drew gregarious Ben's attention, and as soon as he could, at the age of ten, he went to work there. The animal population consisted of dogs for working cattle and dogs who kept the 'coons treed. As Ben grew older he only thought about dogs as he knew them at the farm: they were there to do a job. He even began to see an absurdity in dogs living in houses with people like they had in the posh neighborhoods of San Francisco.

When Ben graduated from high school in 1952, he took his love of animals to the University of California Davis and started in their agricultural sciences program. After a year of study, though, his life took an unexpected turn. When Ben received his draft notice from the Army he didn't think too much about where he would be going or what he would be doing; it was simply a task to be accomplished before he could get back to school and work with animals. When he received word in infantry training that he would be moved to the sentry dog unit at Fort Carson, Colorado, he was excited to at least be working with animals again.

PAULUS

Boulder, Colorado, was a bucolic setting in the 1940s and 1950s. Dean Paulus grew up there in the shadow of the Rockies, on a small wheat farm with mountain meadows spreading all around him. He never knew his birth father, and his mom was always very ill. There wasn't much of a family life for him to speak of, but Paulus's stepfather had a dog that became the boy's constant companion. He wasn't very close to his stepfather. That dog was his family.

When Paulus went to the Army recruiting station in Denver, he was okay with leaving his family behind, but knew that he would miss his canine brother. He went to Fort Ord for basic training and was sent immediately into Light Infantry. A bout of double pneumonia delayed his training, however, setting him back several weeks. Unable to catch up in training, he was washed back into a heavy artillery company. This assignment was a first class ticket to Korea, and for the first time since joining up, he was concerned. Going to fight in Korea was the last thing Paulus had wanted. As it turned out, Heavy Infantry wasn't to be his home, either. At the end of his training he received a different set of orders, changing his course once again.

CHAN

Peter Dak Chan was eight years old in 1940 when his parents escaped the onslaught of the approaching Japanese Army into China, leaving Canton as quickly as they could on a transport ship bound for America. He and his sister, the only two of the family's children to be born in China, roamed the ship on their voyage to Sacramento, California, pretending they were pirates or sailors on an adventure. They never understood the urgency that took them away from China, but they looked forward to the farm paradise they would share with cousins who had gone before them.

Once in California, Chan learned that the American Chinese had fit into a pretty standard track based on white American expectations.

His father told him, "Chinamen do two things in America, cook or hard labor."

Their family worked a farm. All of the children, which eventually became a total of seven siblings, did their part in that enterprise. Chan didn't mind working there, as he knew he wouldn't make much of a cook. His favorite part of the job was tending to the menagerie of animals. They raised meat rabbits and had work horses and farm dogs, and he naturally gravitated to all of them.

But there was also schoolwork to be done, and he liked that as well. Chan learned the nuances of the English language pretty quickly, as his parents had started teaching him English from his infancy. Chan loved math, had a decent understanding of the natural sciences because of his farm life, and loved to play mentally challenging games like chess. His teachers saw a lot of potential in him. When he was in the fifth grade, his teacher offered to take him into her city home, close to a huge variety of educational opportunities, and care for him. His dad refused, stating flatly, "You are a farmer."

In 1953, Chan was drafted at the age of twenty. He was sent to Fort Ord for basic training and knew he was slated for infantry. He also knew that Korea would be his ultimate destination. He never balked at the duty, willing to go wherever he was needed. He struggled, however, with the thought of having to take another person's life. To his relief, a set of orders came down that would change his destiny. He and ten others in his company were being sent to Camp Carson, Colorado, for another mission. The orders read, "8125th Sentry Dog Detachment." Chan was intrigued.

MELOCHICK

Steve Melochick grew up in Pottsville, Pennsylvania, in a home without a lot of love. The day he took the train to his basic training in Camp Gordon, Georgia, he looked out the window at Pottsville and said good-bye forever. He doubted his family would even miss him. He wondered if they even knew he was gone. Then again, they must know. His mother had signed him up early at the age of seventeen. He was the youngest man in his basic training company, and he stood out for all the wrong reasons at a scrawny 105 pounds. The only member of the family Steve was sure he would miss was the family dog.

From basic training Melochick went directly into Explosive Ordnance Disposal (EOD) School, where he would learn to handle enemy explosives on the frontline of war. He knew without question that this would lead him to Korea, and when orders came he was not surprised. He was sent by boat, with what seemed like several thousand other soldiers, to Uijongbu Korea. Not all on board were headed for duty at the ordnance depot, but many in his company were. When he and his fellow trainees from Camp Gordon arrived at their outpost (roughly twenty miles south of the Thirty-Eighth Parallel), they discovered that much of what they had trained for was not in demand there. What the 696th Ordnance Company needed more than actual munitions handlers was security for the ammunition stored there.

Thievery and pilfering by the Koreans was exorbitant in that place, and many of their efforts to thwart it had been ineffectual. Melochick noticed right away that only one program, a new approach to the problem at Uijongbu, was making a difference. The 8125th Sentry Dog Detachment had come there to guard the ammo storage, with great success.[3] Melochick admired the dogs and handlers, but it was the fluid and powerful work of the dogs which most impressed him. Their attentive, loyal behavior made him miss the dog he had left in Pottsville.

SIMPSON

Floyd Simpson grew up on a farm in rural Ohio with three older sisters and one younger brother, his playmates and friends. The farm was full of the traditional menagerie of animals, especially farm dogs.

When Simpson grew up, he volunteered for the draft and chose the Army as his path. He was sent to Fort Ord for basic training. From there he took a different direction than the expected infantry training and volunteered for the Chemical Corps, working with chemical, biological, and radioactive agents. His training took him to Anniston, Alabama. From there a soldier went one of two ways: Germany or Korea. Simpson volunteered for Germany, but being one of the top six in his graduating class earned him guaranteed orders to Korea instead.

Once aboard ship to Korea, Simpson was promptly handed a gun for protection. His commanding officer, a salty colonel, had to look up his military occupational specialty (MOS) because of his unfamiliarity with that line of work. Simpson knew then that he wouldn't be using his education over there. The need for munitions handlers had dwindled. Instead, he was stationed in an ammo depot.

Simpson soon learned that Korea was a dangerous place. It wasn't enemy combatants who threatened security, however, but desperate Koreans who regularly broke into the ammo depot looking for anything of value to steal for their starving families.

OTHER RECRUITS

In this group of new dog handler recruits, nearly eighty men received the call. Not all made it through the process from former infantry to doggie but the ones who did were diverse in every way except their rural upbringing. Slaughter was the only black man in the unit and in a newly integrated Army, stood out to his peers. The Army wasn't trying to fill a quota however; he was chosen for his familiarity with farm life. Wooden hadn't grown up on the family farm, but rather on the glitzy racetracks of California. But he cared for horses from the time he was thirteen and knew a thing or two about training animals. Talley and Batson were the same. Their upbringings had some marker of exposure to animals which the military identified and, as is the Army way, believed that made them good candidates for dog handling. Garfield, who would make it through the training and on to active duty as a working dog handler, was an enigma. His fellow handlers would learn very little about him and would soon see that although he was proficient at doing his job, it was never his desire to do it.

TEAMS

By 1954, roughly eighty men had been diverted from Fort Ord to the upstart sentry dog program at Camp Carson, Colorado. Many of those men would not make it through the program. They ended up back in infantry.

About a hundred dogs awaited their arrival. The dogs almost never left the program, regardless of aptitude. The Army was determined to get everything they could out of their investment. Unfortunately, this meant denying that dogs, just like humans, have their own personalities, uniquely varied from one dog to the next. Some of the K-9 recruits, like their human counterparts, were flexible, teachable, and ready to work. Some would be dragged along to realizing their potential over time. Some would never fully adapt. Yet Army policy put every dog on the scout or sentry track, regardless of whether the dog had the heart or ability for either. As for retirement when the war in Korea was over, the Army would not be returning the dogs to their former owners. Instead, they guaranteed that the dogs would be returned to Camp Carson from wherever they were sent. At least the Army seemed to intend to see the dogs through to the end of their lives.[4]

By the time the men reached the dogs at Carson, the K-9s had been through an extensive selection process. Each had been received at an Army depot for in-processing, where they obtained a Dog Record Card, equivalent to a soldier's Form Twenty (a record of all their processing details). The dogs' records showed the type and number of shots given, physical characteristics, and a personal history. One copy of the record card would accompany the dog wherever it went, another was placed on file in Washington with the Department of the Army, and a third was kept at the place of purchase with the previous owner. Once a dog made it through this process, it would be issued a serial number (like any other soldier) and tattooed on its left flank.[5] This identifying mark effectively made the animal government property.

The personal history of each dog, however, would tell a different story. These living creatures were more than mere pieces of equipment. Some of the men would read the files of their dogs, many of which were once pampered pets now undergoing training to become hardened and ferocious killers. This was cause for some concern, especially at first. Many of the men knew from past experience that if a dog had been properly handled from birth, its instinct was to be a companion to humans, not a foe.

5

GETTING IN

CORPORAL FOWLER

From the beginning of Camp Carson's military working dog program, there was no standard for leadership or organization dedicated to the operations. Men coming into the fledgling program from basic training at Fort Ord often found themselves the ranking man in the company.

A few of them, however, like Corporal Roland Fowler, had some practical experience as leaders in other military career fields. He had earned substantial time-in-grade with the Forty-Seventh Mule Company at Camp Carson, and eventually transferred his experience over to the Doggies. The assumption was if a man could train a mule, he could train a dog. In reality, men like Fowler found in the Doggies a disjointed training protocol and no real plan. The scout dogs, already in place at Camp Carson in 1953, had been semi-established and benefitted from the successes of the Twenty-Sixth Scout Dog Platoon in Korea. The sentry dogs, however, were a rag-tag group of cast-offs—some wash-outs from the scouts and others procured, in a somewhat sloppy way, by the U.S. Quartermaster Corp.[1]

Fowler came to the Camp Carson scout dog program before it even had a name or affiliation. The program had been expanded at Carson from the small Twenty-Sixth Scout Dog Platoon from Fort Riley, and by the time Fowler transitioned there in 1953, there were around eighty scout dogs and twenty handlers in residence. It hadn't been too difficult for Fowler to accept the assignment. Growing up he had loved dogs. In his small Minnesota hometown he had lived the outdoorsman's dream, and dogs had always been a part of that. In fact, he couldn't remember a time that he hadn't had either a pet or a hunting dog at his side—until he joined the Army. His penchant for pastoral life first drew him into the mule company at Carson. In his early years of service, he was able to spend time daily in the mountains with his mule, Jasper, soaking in the Rocky Mountain air. Their regular rides to Pike's Peak were an escape for both of them, and caring for Jasper gave Fowler a connection to home. But an incident beyond his control would lead to his next great adventure with the dogs.

Although he never skipped grooming or picking Jasper's hooves, the mule was prone to injury and illness. Fowler believed Jasper went looking for ways to injure himself on a daily basis. Shortly after Fowler rode Jasper in the 1952 Armed Forces Parade in Colorado Springs, the mule developed a case of road-founder that would force the Army to pull him from service indefinitely. He had been properly shod, and Fowler had checked his hooves thoroughly before ever getting in the saddle. Most likely Jasper's love of sweet feed had caused his joints to fail, but in the Army way, someone had to bear the blame. Fowler received a demotion to stockade guard.

Fowler's brief stint at the stockade didn't work out, either. In a confusing incident he discharged his weapon at a detainee. He missed, likely on purpose, but nevertheless ended up looking for another job. There weren't too many more places to fall from the humiliating work of guarding drunks and petty offenders in the stockade, but the Army decided to give him a choice: the icy frozen tundra of Alaska or Mary Ellen Ranch in nearby Camp Carson to work as a scout dog handler.

The dogs were the natural choice.

When Fowler came into the scout dog platoon, there were twenty handlers as well as rank-structured leadership. They were a somewhat experienced unit, and their training was on point. Fowler couldn't believe how wonderful the dogs were at their jobs. The precision of their "hunt" reminded him of his favorite hunting dogs back home. These dogs lived for their daily games of hide-and-seek and relished the praise of their handlers for making a good find. Often, a decoy (usually a soldier borrowed from the nearby infantry platoon) would be set 1,400 yards away, and the dogs could find him before the platoon's lieutenant even got to the field. Once, their lieutenant came out to observe and asked Fowler, "When are you going to start?" The dogs had already made ten captures, twenty minutes before his arrival.

Fowler's scout dog became his faithful companion. Smokey was a beautiful German Shepherd, with grey coat and dark eyes, and he loved his job. He had an incredibly proficient nose and was able to find a man in seconds instead of minutes. On every find, Smokey would look to Fowler for praise. An exuberant utterance of "Good boy!" was the only reward used in the early training of military working dogs, and Smokey worked hard to earn it. Man and dog spent more than half of every day together, and the bond they formed was unbreakable. Fowler could say, after only a short few weeks of training together, that he loved Smokey more than most people—like family and even more.

Although there was structured leadership on the scout dog training side, there was very little in the sentry dog program. Fowler had established himself in the scout dog program as a trustworthy leader and was in line to make sergeant soon. He received orders to the 8125th Sentry Dog Detachment in the beginning of 1954 and reluctantly handed Smokey's leash to another handler. He knew he could trust Smokey to this new handler: the young man had already expressed a love for the dog more than once. At the 8125th Fowler's mission would be very different and far more complicated. The sentries needed his experience.

The Doggies were going to Korea.

EARLY FRIENDSHIPS

The boys assessed each other, sizing each other up by what they already knew from time together at Fort Ord. The bus ride had given them time to pick each other apart, in a soldier's way, finding out who was sensitive about what and how far the teasing could go. They pushed each other's buttons in those confined hours on the road—and quickly amalgamated into certain friendships. They had no idea that these friendships would last a lifetime.

Even before they reached the gates at Carson, a unity had emerged that only shared suffering could create. The drudgery of duty, the uncertainty of success at their jobs, the physical rigors of military life had all been a part of their shared experience so far. But their shared unspoken fear of the unknown, hovering just over their heads, would cause them to lean on each other in ways they had never leaned on another human being before.

Fickes was the baby of the bunch and still full of wide-eyed optimism. His eyes sparkled with laughter, and he quickly became a general favorite with his little brother antics. He played along and told everyone that he had shaved for the first time when he went to basic. Everyone readily believed him—he was scrawny, fresh-faced, and awkward. His youth was endearing, though, and many of the men took to him immediately. Some would eventually take him under their wing as though he was their own kid brother. It also helped his popularity that Fickes could play the ukulele and had a fairly extensive knowledge of the Burl Ives songbook.

Broadway was the Texan of the group, a larger-than-life character, six feet tall. Naturally, the guys started calling him "Tex." Tex hit it off right away with Chan, his frequent KP buddy. Chan was probably a foot shorter than Tex, and the two of them were quite a pair. The very first night they got stuck in the kitchen together, making breakfast for all the new arrivals at the 8125th. Chan confided in Tex that he hoped they weren't destined for Korea—as he expressed it, he didn't have a "Chinaman's chance of surviving it." Tex urged him to relax. He did his best to distract him with stories about Texas, its vast space, beautiful women, and giant people.

Chan didn't even flinch when Tex and the others started calling him "Chin" (as if they couldn't read the nametape on the uniform). He was the kind of guy who took it all in stride. His spirit was generous and easygoing, and he didn't have the heart to hurt anyone's feelings. Besides, Chan had learned to deal with stereotypes Chinese people endured in the country from his first arrival on these shores. Being Asian brought scrutiny on his family for generations. The untrained eye saw him as a Japanese boy, the enemy, during World

War II, and that same untrained eye thought he might be the new enemy, Korean, now that he was a man. And although he was as American in every way as the soldier next to him, he had to prove that his customs weren't as foreign as everyone assumed.

Slaughter sat quietly on the bus, uniform on point. He was the only black man in the unit, and he felt isolated in this newly integrated Army.[2] The others knew Slaughter's standards were exacting, and his appearance was important to him. They figured he felt he had some-thing to prove. As a result, he escaped most of the collective bullying, even the good-natured kind. Poole was one of the few guys that Slaughter immediately let into his fold. They had a natural rapport and would remain close. Paulus and Poole also hit it off, naturally drawing Slaughter into the circle.

Batson was a quiet Midwestern boy with a pleasant expression and generally jovial disposition.

Wooden was stoic—his expression was pleasant enough that no one considered him troublesome, only somewhat mysterious. He had grown up around animals, jockeying racehorses in his teen years, and possessed a cool confidence that few dared to transgress.

Hatch was a jokester, his repertoire of dirty jokes plentiful. He entered the group like a court jester, which effectively earned him a position of favor with everyone. It probably struck many as odd that this Mormon boy had such a quick wit and saucy humor, but he wielded it to catch them off-guard and win them over.

Rath came off very talkative. He was a Germanic Nebraska boy, rooted in his conservative heritage and Christian faith. The boys tested him at first to see how strict he really was. They picked at him to elicit the slightest blush. He passed the test by smiling at all the appropriate places.

Bakken, having grown up in the same area with many of the same values, didn't come off with the same precocious nature. But Bakken and Rath hit it off in spite of their very different personalities. A third eventually joined their sub-group of friends. Stalke easily fit into the group, and a friendship was born that would last for a very long time. Peterson and Munson were also reunited with Bakken and flowed easily into the new group of friends.

Jellison mixed readily among most of the men, easily befriending them. Stewart was like a young pup, heartily chatting everyone up. Both received their fair share of ribbing, but like the rest of the guys they soon found a balance of acceptability.

Garfield seemed like he might be the only loose cannon in the bunch. His habits hinted at an attitude more serious than mischievousness.

The friendships between these men, formed quickly, would be critical to the success of this unit. Yet as they drove up to the gates of

Fickes and Chan formed a lifelong friendship early on.

Camp Carson, none of them had any idea how deep a friendship could really be.

CAMP CARSON

The dogs at Camp Carson had come from all over the country, just like the men, and they now sat in their kennels eager to address the new scents hanging in the air. They had already gone through their in-processing and basic, like the men, and were awaiting the arrival of new handlers. They anxiously pranced around in anticipation of their new pack leaders.

The 8125th Sentry Dog Detachment was a catch-all for unclassifiable dogs. Some of the dogs had washed out of scout training due to their inability to keep quiet. Barkers need not apply to be scout dogs, as the element of surprise was key to a scout's success. Others had been sent directly to the sentry unit because the need for scouts in Korea had waned after they had already been purchased. All the dogs had gone through basic obedience, some even before they became soldiers. The dogs lived according to established routines of training, grooming, feeding, and petting, but that routine had recently lapsed in the days before the bus pulled up to the gates at Carson. Now the dogs could sense their beloved jobs would start again soon.

In the distance the men saw the kennels and heard the high yips. Without even laying eyes on the dogs, their souls were stirred by the ancient calling together of the pack.[3] The men glanced at each other, sharing the same thought: "I want to meet my dog."

Just as the men felt the energy of the pending meetings between K-9 and soldier, the dogs also felt it—maybe even on a higher level. Their extrasensory abilities had alerted them to changes many days before, and they were frenetic.[4] They had already been through handlers and done the work of a military working dog by now, but few had formed bonds. For the dogs who had washed out from the scout division, their previous handlers would have spent just enough time with them to find out they were not scout material. The dogs who were never even considered for scouts had gone through a fair amount of basic obedience handling. All the dogs, having come from private homes, had known the bond between a man and a dog in their former lives, and each was longing for that bond again.

THE DOGS

The dogs came in many marking variations of the German Shepherd breed color standard: tan, white, and black. Their personalities also varied widely. Some were playful goofballs, while others were timid. Some would roll over for a scratch on the belly, while others would raise hackles at just a passing glance.

Many of them had been given names that implied something about their character, like Chief, Bullet, Junker, and Spooks. A lot of the dogs had been given names that reflected their pedigreed German ancestry: Duke, Rex, Lutz, Stagmar, Rommel, Fritz, and Prinz. Some dogs were just given good, old-fashioned dog "handles," such as Willy, Tex, Chito, Wolf, and Grey.

Duke was a veteran in his own right. A beautiful German Shepherd of just the right proportions, he had come to Camp Carson at the age of six. By dog measures he was middle-aged. He had come from a kennel owned by an "F. W. Keesee" in Falls Church, Virginia, not long before the men were to arrive. Apparently his advanced age didn't hinder his ability to "learn new tricks"—everyone who came in contact with him described him as "smart as hell." Like many of the dogs, Duke loved the games the Army had designed for them.

Duchess was one of the few females at Camp Carson. Most remained back home in their respective kennels to continue breeding lines. Duchess quickly gained a reputation for "bitchiness," a beneficial trait in the sentry dog world.

Prinz sat quietly chained to his dog house, an experience he hadn't known in his former life. Still, he was happy, his usual countenance shining through in spite of the change of scenery. Routine was good for him. The regular walks and daily grooming pleased him, and the food was exquisite. Horse meat and Wheaties seemed a world away from the dry kibble he had known with Gerry. Aside from the train ride in the big crate, everything seemed pretty close to normal for Prinz. All that was lacking now was the fading aroma of Gerry. It still permeated slightly. He even thought he might know the way home, following that faint, wafting memory, if he tried. But Prinz decided to ride it out. There were new smells in this place that he couldn't discredit. He decided he would see what that was all about.

The men disembarked at their barracks to meet Corporals Brandenburg, Talley, and Fowler, and the unit's OIC, Lieutenant Zach Word. They had hoped to meet the dogs right away, but their hopes were immediately dashed: it would be days before they could meet the dogs, and even that was contingent on everything falling in line.

Fowler explained to them that this was a painstaking process. The men had to build trust with the dogs, and it couldn't be done in a day. "Settle in for the night," he ordered. "Private Chan, pick a buddy and make the guys some chow. Tomorrow you will start getting to know your dogs on paper, and there's a lot to learn. Be ready."

Chan looked at Broadway and smiled. "You're with me, Tex!"

Broadway feigned irritation. "Why the hell do I have to do it? Of course they need a Chinaman to cook, but why me?"

Chan asked if Broadway knew how to cook eggs.

"Well of course I can!" Broadway replied. "Best damn eggs on earth!"

"Good," Chan grinned. "I'll peel the potatoes."

BONDING

Falge had been at Carson for some time before the other guys arrived. He had flown into Colorado Springs from Fort Ord and was immediately struck by the beautiful mountains spiraling upward around him. He took note of a sign introducing the city as the "Future Home of the United States Air Force Academy." Carson was set in classic Colorado ranch country, which lent itself well to a place where dogs and horses roamed. He thought what a shame it would be for urban sprawl to take over.

At first Falge had been assigned to the scout dogs. He loved the work there and found the dogs to be different from any he had ever known before. They seemed smart. Not that the dogs he had known before weren't, but these dogs seemed to have an added dimension to their personalities. Their job had given them an added vocabulary. The dogs moved silently in their play and work, coursing through the high desert plains of Colorado, finding first one objective and then the next.[5] Falge admired their drive and determination.

When he transferred to work with the sentry dogs, he quickly learned the dogs were just as clever on that side of the compound. He soon formed a bond of trust with his companion dog, Stagmar, as she showed herself to be capable of protecting him.

Benevenga, or as the men called him, "Ben," had been with Falge in the scouts and was, by all accounts, a great dog handler. His fellow soldiers loved working with him because he clearly loved his work with the dogs. More than that, Ben had a connection to the dogs

Falge and sentry dog Lutz take a break from training at Camp Carson.

which few could claim. It was the procedure to "square your dog" in formation by making the dog sit on a certain point, next to the handler, in an erect and alert position. Ben could get his dog in that position easily, and if the dog strayed a millimeter, Ben could "ask" him to shift his butt with a look alone. The other guys often sat in awe of that, resigning themselves to the idea that that is something one is born with, not something developed. Ben was a very humble guy, though, and many of them found it hard to get to know him. He simply didn't like to talk about himself. Falge, however, being Ben's constant bunkmate (most likely a result of their names being so close, alphabetically, on the roster) got to know Ben well, and they were good friends.

When Ben received word that he would be going to the sentry dog side, he looked forward to the challenge of working new dogs. He was also glad to be going along with his buddy Falge. But he was

"Ben" and Falge relax with Falge's dog Stagmar.

pretty sure that the sentries could never match the prowess of the scout dogs who had been trained to do stealthy work across enemy lines. "It's just a job," he thought and moved on in military fashion.

The first night the men arrived at the 8125th, Falge and Ben were there waiting. As the men gathered around to eat their late-night chow, they were full of questions for the veterans. What were the dogs like? What was their mission? What would their training be like? Falge answered their questions as best he could, but he advised them the only thing they needed to worry about was "getting in" on their dog. Benevenga was asked what his dog was like, to which Falge replied, "Vicious as hell."

The morning after their arrival, and much to the men's frustration, they learned they would not be meeting the dogs right away. In spite of their disappointment, many took comfort in at least learning their dogs' names. Each man would be paired with one dog, but they all would be asked to handle more than one dog from time to time. Further, there were some shared responsibilities in caring for the dogs. For the most part, however, the method of partnership between one man and one dog, which had been proven so effective during World War II, would continue in the Army's K-9 training program.

Falge was paired with Stag. Fickes got Duke. Broadway had the flop-eared Rex, tattoo # E248, a dog he described as "unable to win any beauty contests but smart." Slaughter was paired with the striking Jet, a silky-coated, black Shepherd. Hatch was teamed with Willy. Rath would be with Fritz. Bakken got Bullet. Stahlke went with Junker. Laidback Jellison got a matching dog in Tex. Stewart got

Bakken and Bullet.

Rath and Fritz.

high-strung Duchess. Benevenga had Grey. Paulus paired with Fritz, a super witty dog and an excellent example of the German Shepherd breed standard. Wooden had the prey-driven Chief. Batson teamed up with Chito. Peterson got arguably one of the most vicious dogs in the bunch, Wolf. The effervescent Chan was matched with an equally happy dog, Prinz.

Before meeting the dogs face-to-face, each man got to look at his dog's dossier. The files on most included extensive medical histories, as well as the point of receipt for the dogs. There were training records as well, giving the men an idea of how to approach their dogs by adjusting for temperament. They also learned what, how much, and how often the dogs ate. The thing consistently lacking in these records, however, was a backstory. Most men would never know who their dogs had been in civilian life.

Slaughter and Jet.

Stahlke and Junker.

Prinz was the exception.

That same day, Lieutenant Word called Chan into the office. Chan was pretty sure the lieutenant had something to say about chow the night before—or maybe he planned to assign him some other "Chinaman's" duty, like laundry. He was relieved and even a little flattered to learn the OIC wanted to talk to him about his dog.

"Private Chan, I have a letter for you," Word said. "This letter is from sixteen-year-old Mary Jay Osler of Bangor, Maine. She writes to say that that dog means the world to her. She requests that she be informed about Prinz's actions, and because we are determined to keep a positive relationship with community, we will go above and beyond to make that happen. Do you understand that, Private Chan?"

Chan smiled. "Of course, sir." As he walked out of the office, staring at the letter, he thought he smelled perfume coming from the envelope.

> To Whom It May Concern,
>
> My name is Mary Jay Osler. I am a 16-year-old high school student from Bangor Maine. I love theater (I'm an actress), history, going to the drive-in with my friends, and dogs. Prinz is such a good boy and I've spent lots of time with him. I was really sad to lose him but I am proud of the service he and you are giving to the country. I would love to hear about his adventures. Will you write to me and let me know how he's doing in his training?
>
> Sincerely,
> Mary Jay

An actress? Chan was pretty sure she must be a looker. Oh yeah, he would write and write often. It was too bad he didn't know much more about Prinz from the letter, but he hoped she would write more in future letters about his dog.

It was a big day when the men finally met their dogs, a few days later. The kennels were busy with excitement. There was no formula for "getting in." The men had been briefed on that fact. The introduction was critical, and if it took days to achieve, they could take that time. Trust must be the cornerstone of an everlasting bond between man and dog, and it could never be rushed. Each man gauged his dog's behavior and adjusted accordingly. Some dogs were easy. Saddling up to them, gently chirping their name, and slipping the choke chain on worked right away. Others snarled, gnashed teeth, and lashed out at the end of their chains.

Stewart had one of the more difficult dogs. He spent many sweaty, wide-eyed hours getting close to Duchess. Oddly, when he did finally get the choke chain on, she could be as gentle as they came, and proficient at the job of obedience. Still, he learned never to turn his back on her because of her reputation. Later he would remember that once, when a dust storm kicked up across the Colorado desert, he kicked Duchess out of her dog house and climb inside to protect himself. He felt it was justified for all the times she had spun and bitten his leg.

Obedience was their first work together, and the dogs had already been put through rigorous training. It was the men who had to learn to consistently give the command and expect one hundred percent compliance. Sometimes, the seasoned K-9s would take advantage of their rookie partners and pretend that they were also newbies. This is where extreme patience came into play for the handlers. The dogs were never to be disciplined with force or aggression. Neither were they ever given food rewards or toys. The best and most consistent way for the dogs to learn their jobs was with praise and affection. This was one of the hardest aspects of aggression training with the dogs. When a dog lashed out at a handler—and it happened fairly often with some dogs—the handler had to reward the behavior, against all instincts. The ultimate goal of the praise-reward system was to have the dog trust only its handler. No one was supposed to give praise to a dog that wasn't his own.

Aggression training consisted of work with a leather collar and leash and the "game" of running away. The men would take turns donning a bite-suit—a super heavy insulated cotton duck pants and shirt combination, which offered no protection for the head and neck—and acting as bait for the dogs. Sometimes the aggressor would poke at the dog with a stick or move suddenly towards the handler. The aggressor would repeat the behavior until the dog showed some sort of irritation with the action, which would be the root of aggression. When the slightest irritation did arise, the handler would praise the dog. Broadway referred to it as "making the dog feel like the big man on campus." As the dogs began to become more agitated over time, the handlers began tapping into their natural prey drive and encouraging them to take down a fleeing man. The dogs could never be outrun. For the handlers, the key was controlling the instinct they had uncovered. In time, and with training, the dogs eventually learned to release bite pressure when the assailant stopped struggling. With precise timing, the handlers were able to tell the dogs, "off," and the dogs would release completely. This was never perfect, as some dogs began to really enjoy their work and had a hard time releasing. Sometimes the man in the bite suit would be taken down like a running deer and shaken like a rabbit.

Peterson's dog, Wolf (tattoo #E374), never made a distinction between his handler and an assailant. Peterson described his difficulty simply: "Well it took a while to get a hold of that one." Wolf was ferocious, and Peterson never knew when he might turn and get him instead of the bad guy. This extreme aggression, however, was preferential in the Army's criteria for a sentry dog. Peterson just had to learn to live with and manage Wolf. Through training, he was able to foresee the potential for a bite and do whatever he could to avoid it. But Peterson saw the wounds inflicted by Wolf as just another part of the job description. His perpetually bandaged legs and arms drew excessive mockery from the other guys. Peterson would laugh it off. "The Army wants 'em mean, and I'm here to serve."[6]

Many of the dogs, not naturally prone to being aggressive toward people, would only associate the game with the suit. Fickes's dog, Duke, known for his gregarious love of people, didn't have much of a heart for sentry work. The others often called him a "pussycat." But with training, Fickes was able to prove that he could attack. When the suit went on, Duke would get after it. One day Fickes came around the corner with Duke and discovered someone had left the bite suit on the ground. Duke flew into a rage at the site of the thing, grabbed it up, and shook it with vigor. Fickes marveled at the animal's raw aggression and rage. He thought to himself, "Now if I can just get the enemy to wear the suit at all times, I should be safe." Fickes ultimately trusted Duke, however, because he saw the dog's desire to please him. "He's not a dumb animal," he told the guys. "In fact, truth be told, Duke is more soldier than I'll ever be."

Chan and Prinz went through all the same training as Fickes and Duke, but with a different result. At the end of training, even after Prinz was deemed fit for duty, Chan found himself afraid of his dog—not his aggression, but his half-hearted at attacks. Chan was never sure if Prinz would protect him from a real threat. Prinz, however, enjoyed the game and looked forward to the time spent with his handler every day. He worked hard to make him happy. And Chan returned daily, so Prinz figured he must be playing the game right.

Over the course of ten weeks of training, the men and dogs worked very closely together, spending very little time apart. The men would occasionally get town passes and take a few hours away from the dogs. Falge and Benevenga liked to go ice skating at the Broadmoor Hotel, and many of the guys cruised around town to mingle with the local ladies. Bar-hopping was pretty popular for the soldiers at Camp Carson, but many bars discriminated against them. Hatch once found a local Colorado Springs bar with a sign in the window, reading, "No soldiers, niggers, or dogs allowed." The married guys like Jellison and Talley preferred to stick together in their down time. They tried to stay out of trouble and avoid the reputation soldiers could get from too much leisure. Garfield, however, cared very little about reputation. The guys always knew he was up for anything if the mood hit them.

On August 16, 1954, fifty-one men were awarded the Primary Military Occupational Specialty (MOS) 3458, making them Military Working Dog Handlers. Although they were carrying out Military Police duties in their sentry work, they were not actual MPs. They were, instead, a select and specialized group of men who weren't acting alone. Their dogs were their partners, working alongside them in dangerous situations. In the long training hours spent together, the men and K-9s had bonded, learning every nuance of their counterparts. The dogs knew their handlers by the slightest expression, inflection of voice, or flick of the wrist. The handlers knew their dogs through grooming, working, and feeding, and could detect even the slightest sign of trouble. They trusted each other. The men had seen that the dogs were willing to lay down their lives for the handlers without hesitation. They felt the same way, now, about their dogs.

Soon enough, orders came down for the 8125th to head to a "secret location in the far east." The men were told to pack up their equipment for mobility. The dogs were listed on their orders as their primary equipment. The Army viewed the dogs differently than the handlers did—the handlers saw their dogs as partners. The Army saw the dogs as tools for accomplishing a mission.

6

SECRET DEPLOYMENT

Everything was loaded onto a train bound for the West Coast. The men had received pre-deployment vaccinations, and the dogs had, too, which was odd. The men bold enough to inquire learned that men and dogs were being vaccinated for diseases virtually unheard of in the United States. These inoculations were particular to Third World countries and specific to Asia. That was far from promising. Up until that point the men had been hopeful that their mission might take them to Germany. Upon embarkation, many still wondered if they might be bound for Japan, but occupation and reconstruction there had ended two years before; Japan had very little need for sentries. It was a long shot, but one that many of the guys were clinging to.

The dogs had special wooden crates for shipping, just like the ones the Army had built to bring them to Carson from their respective homes. The crates were small, and the 90 to 100 pound dogs barely had room to turn around. Each crate was stamped with the dog's serial number, but no name. They were loaded onto a train car together so the men could easily gain access to them and relieve them at each stop. The dogs' car was closer to the cargo area than the passenger cars where the men traveled. As they rode west through the Rockies, many of the men wondered if their dogs were well and worried about them overheating in an unventilated boxcar, baked in the late August sun. They all agreed that they would get to the dogs as soon as possible, but that would be several hours away, in Billings, Montana.

When they finally pulled into Billings, the men were eager to get to their dogs, their minds full of the task at hand: feed, water, and walk. If they could get some exercise in for the dogs' tired minds and cramped bodies, too, that would be optimal. As they approached the platform, however, ready to get to work, they saw what might be a potential problem. The area was full of people, waving flags and holding welcome signs. Someone had alerted the sleepy town of Billings that some celebrities were coming to town—the dogs.

A reporter from the *Billings Gazette* met the awe-struck passengers as they stepped off the train. Pad and pen in hand, he wanted to know about their mission, their objective, their training. The guys were trying desperately to get to the dogs and make sure they were okay, but the reporter was persistent.

"Can I meet your dog, soldier?" he chirped.

The guys agreed that as soon as they made sure the dogs were comfortable, they could meet—though they knew the reporter had no idea what he was in for. The reporter followed behind, bouncing with excitement. But as the doors to the boxcar were flung open, the reporter stopped dead in his tracks. The blood-curdling snarls and snaps told the reporter these were not sweet puppies, but war machines. He stepped back gingerly and let the GIs get to their K-9s.

The water placed in the crates for each dog had carried them through, and the dogs were all well—and thoroughly irritated. They relieved themselves all around the train station as civilians looked on, awestruck by the simultaneous power and gentleness of the dogs. Some of the bystanders who asked to pet the dogs were met with a tail-wagging, generous response. Other dogs weren't approachable, and the threat of snapping jaws kept onlookers at bay. The single guys couldn't help but notice all the fresh-faced bobby-soxers who showed a keen interest in their dogs. The ones with aggressive dogs used it to their advantage, flexing muscle over agitated dogs and preening for the ladies. Some of the guys may even have agitated their dogs for just that purpose. Those with the more docile dogs also capitalized by encouraging the dogs to stand for petting and hugs. Prinz and Duke loved the attention, and Chan and Fickes were grateful for once for their dogs being the docile house pets they were at heart.

There was some time left before the train departed after the dogs had been tended to, and the civilian crowd pushed the handlers for a demo of what the dogs could do. Paulus and Poole had exceptional dogs and loved to show them off, so they agreed. Fowler also joined in, using whatever dog was nearby. He had the uncanny ability to "get in" on all the dogs. Slaughter's dog, Jet, was a showboat as he always kept his beautiful coat immaculate. The crowds were thrilled with the prowess of these military working dogs and a sense of pride seemed to waft over everyone there. This was heartening for the men. Already in their relatively short military careers, the men had often experienced apathy among civilians for their Army mission. In this little town, though, the people were thrilled by what handlers and dogs were doing for their country. Besides, a lot of folks there agreed, it's hard not to love a beautiful dog.

After the demo, the men still had some time to kill before the train moved on. Some girls offered to show them the highlights of Billings. They were excited to spend some time with pretty girls, not knowing when this opportunity might arise again, but they couldn't take the dogs with them. They debated putting the dogs back in their kennels prematurely, but in the end it was a sacrifice most of them made. This was the first time any of them had left their dogs for a significant amount of time since training began. Many of the guys were unable to enjoy themselves, because they were too worried about their dogs. Fowler told some of the guys he felt like he was "leaving part of myself behind." Several came back to the train earlier than necessary to check on the dogs.

The next morning, the train rambled westward. Conversation about their ultimate destination was on the forefront. Chan was sure they were going to Japan. Hatch hoped the same. Their orders were "top secret," however, which, as the men talked it over, implied somewhere less benign. They knew they would have another chance to stretch their legs, dogs and men together, at the Seattle pier, before boarding a ship bound for somewhere in the Far East. The dogs would have to be boarded with all the accompanying supplies. There were barrels of horse meat, veterinary supplies, and training aids to labor over. The men had also seen what was brought from the armory; each would be issued a .45 ACP M1911. They tabled their thoughts about going where a pistol would be necessary and talked instead about their dogs. Although Hatch was bemused and Falge said he was a little apprehensive, both agreed they were probably making more of the situation than necessary. All the men in ear shot agreed that the dogs had their backs.

Chan loudly announced, "Anyway, I'd rather have the dog than the pistol any day."

"Why's that Chin?" Hatch chuckled.

Chan shot back, "Cause the dog don't miss!"

A few days later, the men and dogs arrived at the Seattle Port of Embarkation. Just like at Billings, reporters crowded around the men, and the dogs were taken out of their kennels and brought around for photo opportunities. The next day they would be boarded onto the fantail of the ship, in the same crates they had been in throughout their Army careers, and sent to their destination. There would be no downtime in Seattle for the men, although the reporters would go on to describe this moment as "leisurely."[1] Really, the media wasn't much interested in the handlers. The men's names had to be withheld from the public because of the mission's top secret classification, and they really weren't the "human interest" story the media wanted, anyway. The dogs were the stars of the show. Camera bulbs flashed and popped as the handlers lined them up, put them in a "sit and stay," and posed.

The Army's Public Relations Department relished the attention because, in spite of the viciousness they had encouraged in the dogs, it was beneficial to them to put a benevolent face—or snout—on the mission about to be undertaken. Further, it was a historical point of interest that these were the first "K-9 warriors" through Seattle since World War II.[2]

Once packed back into their cramped quarters on the fantail of the USS *W.H. Gordon*, the dogs yipped and whined.[3] The salty air and smell of the sea were very different from their last home in Colorado, and they called to each other for acknowledgment and affirmation that the security of the pack was still intact. Prinz settled easier than most. His good nature made him consistently even-keeled. Chan was in and out of the dog's area throughout the loading process, and he walked by Prinz's kennel often. Prinz reveled in his familiar scent, and he felt settled knowing his beloved handler was nearby. He shifted his weight inside his box, spun, and lay down with his back to the door. No need, he thought, to be on guard as long as Chan was on duty.

The men look across the ocean, anticipating the journey of a lifetime.

Above deck the men were finally settling in, too. Chan and Broadway had KP duty once again and had loaded 200 pounds of potatoes for fifty-six men. At least they would have enough to eat. Besides eating, there were other ways to combat boredom on the ship. One of their favorite amusements was to let the sailors aboard get too close to the dogs. This turned the necessary exercise time for the dogs into a sport for the handlers. It didn't take too long for the sailors to figure it out, though, so the men had to devise new entertainment.

Chan pours water out aboard ship to bring to the thirsty dogs below.

The handlers still did not know where they were going, but there were plenty of rumors and whisperings of where they were headed. Benevenga was the only one who was completely certain they were going to be assigned duty in Japan.

A couple days into their voyage, Paulus burst into the berthing area. "I just heard a sailor say we're headed for Sasebo, Japan!"

"Hot damn, I told you," Benevenga blurted.

Fickes was excited. "I bet Chin can get us some girls!"

"That's Japan. I'm Chinese." Chan was not amused.

Someone asked the question, "What are the dogs gonna do?" The question was glossed over and eventually lost in the collective sense of relief that they weren't going to Korea.

Later, Broadway heard Lieutenant Word tell one of the men that they were headed to someplace that started with a "K." Thinking of his Bluegrass home, the soldier joked, "Oh, we're going back to Kentucky!"

Chan sat down to compose a letter. With fresh news in hand, he felt like he could finally tell Mary Jay something substantial. Of course he had kept her apprised of Prinz's training at Carson, but nothing with detail. He remarked that Prinz was a sweet dog (hoping that she wouldn't read between the lines to see "kind of hopeless as a sentry"), and that he was coming along.

Dear Mary Jay,

Today we boarded a ship in Seattle and we are headed to the Far East. I'm not supposed to discuss our exact destination, for matters of operational security, but I can tell you that we will be in a nice place where Prinz will live a life of doggie luxury. I was wondering, can you send me a picture of you?

Pete

Two days into their voyage, the men were called together for a briefing. They learned that although they would be stopping in Japan to resupply, the men and dogs would not be going ashore. Instead, they were moving on to Incheon, Korea, where rioting had become a problem after UN resolutions and sanctions had left the country bereft of aid. Because of the conflict, many in that country were homeless and starving. The country had been looted and burned; stripped of all natural resources which could provide for a hungry people. Further, American military posts were being invaded and robbed of all resources by desperate Koreans. And although some pockets of hostility from the enemy remained a problem for the United States military personnel there, it was the dogs' role to control riots (just their presence was threatening enough to many Koreans) and to protect property that proved an invaluable asset to our nation's interests.

As the ship rolled on to Japan, the men, now certain of their final destination, looked at their dogs in a different light. If they hadn't been completely grateful before, now they saw their dogs as the lifelines they truly were. The situation was terrible, any way you looked at it. "The enemy" they were about to face would be someone who wanted to survive, someone who needed desperately to eat. They would not be facing hardened warriors who had been trained to kill, but overwrought parents who needed to feed famished mouths and quiet empty bellies. Many of the men had experienced poverty and believed they could wrap their heads around the situation. But for many of the men, the mission conflicted painfully with the charitable ideals that had been instilled in them by hardworking, Christian, small-town parents. Their fears of going to Korea were now realized in a more profound way.

The dogs had demonstrated their ability to kill a man. In the bite suit the men had experienced for themselves the power of those iron jaws and sharp teeth. They also understood that the struggle in Korea could very easily come down to nothing more than kill or be killed. The men had been told in the briefing that they must try to call the dogs off once a suspect was subdued, but they also understood that if a perpetrator continued to struggle, the situation might go beyond the handler's control. They had learned the commands in English, but now they also learned how to say "Stop resisting" in Korean. Lieutenant Word told the men he would buy a case of beer or a fifth of liquor for any suspect apprehended, "dead or alive." The men took this to mean they would be asked to set their personal values aside for the Army mission. Each man would wrestle with that from then on.

The dogs were a lifeline, and the men understood that well. They had always taken great care of the dogs but now, more than ever, their diligence in caring for them was amplified. Through typhoons and treacherous seas, the men made sure the dogs were properly exercised and fed aboard ship. The dogs would sometimes be staked out on the ship's deck so they could use muscles that might atrophy sitting in the kennels all day. The dogs' daily rations were fortified, but only enough to encourage lean, powerful muscle mass. Regularly the men checked for any sign of illness or injury that might prevent the dogs from performing at their optimum capability.

The 8125th was aboard ship for twenty-two days before landing at Incheon. The smell was overpowering from two miles out. To the men it was a rancid stench of rot and sewage. For the dogs it must have been overpowering. They became anxious when the kennels were brought above deck. Many of the dogs shivered and whined inside their kennels, while others raised hackles and growled.

Hatch and Stewart thought the dogs might just have a built-in loathing for Koreans, their enemy in this game. Chan told them if it was Asians the dogs hated, he would have been eaten long ago. Hatch had heard a story from someone who had gone to Korea before: "If you let the dogs lick up what's left of a blown-up Korean, you'll have the meanest dog you've ever seen!" The consensus among the men, however, was that the dogs could certainly smell, even two miles out, the rot in the Korean gut of dogs the people had eaten before.

Landing barges came out to meet the men and dogs, anchored a half-mile off shore and bring them in across twenty-foot swells. The dogs would stay in their shipping crates, to keep them safe from being jostled out of the boats into the treacherous water, until finally being unloaded in their permanent location. They were divided among four locations: Siheung with the Fifty-Eighth Ordnance Co., Yong Dong Po, Musan-ni, and Uijongbu with the 696th Ordinance Co.

The men were divided among these four locations too, meaning they would be separated from each other for the first time since training began. Over time they found out that they would rotate between posts, but close friendships were divided nonetheless. The men were grateful, however, knowing they would always have their dogs by their sides.

Many were still fearful of the assignment. Hatch was one of them. On land in Incheon, the men were briefed by a colonel who told them their mission had been planned a year before their arrival. He showed them on the map where the action had been in relation to where they were going. Seeing the fear in his eyes, the colonel asked Hatch if he was afraid.

"Hell yes!" Hatch was being honest.

"Good," the colonel retorted. "You'll stay awake then."

Chan was one of the soldiers whose job it was to unload the dog crates from the barge onto the awaiting convoy of deuce-and-half trucks. When Prinz was unloaded he caught Chan's eyes and happily wagged his tail at his old friend. Yet Chan's face looked somehow unfamiliar to Prinz.

"Damn, Prinz, you're a little too happy." It was disappointment that Prinz had registered in his handler's face.

Chan pulled King's crate off next and placed him next to Prinz. An unwitting Korean civilian walked by, and King flew into a barking, frothing rage at the sight of him. Prinz looked around, trying to process the mood of the pack, taking into consideration Chan's lack of reaction and King's excessive one. After assessing the scene, Prinz decided Chan was his leader, and his instinct was the right one. He laid down and didn't pay the passerby any further mind. Then, something odd happened. Chan went to King and called him a "good boy."

"Awww Prinz, don't get your feelings hurt," Chan joked. He turned to Broadway, who was standing close by, and asked about King. It turns out King was one of the dogs who hadn't been paired with just one handler. He could be rotated in on the off-time of other dedicated dogs.

The one thing Chan had dreaded most about assignment in Korea was the thought of having to kill someone. He had prepared himself for the possibility of letting a dog loose that might, in turn, kill someone if it couldn't be called off. But he hoped that just the threat of a vicious dog would be enough to thwart the enemy. The Korean civilian who had just walked by was in a puddle of terror from King's reaction, and the men knew that this, in general, was the way most Koreans would react. They were terrified of the dogs.

"I'll be taking King on patrol," Chan told Broadway. King's bark was all he would need to get through the next sixteen months.

The men headed out to their respective areas, in their respective vehicles loaded with dogs and supplies. Stewart, Hatch, Falge, Paulus, Rath, Stahlke, Jellison, and Poole went initially to Uijongbu. Broadway, Chan, Fickes, and Benevenga went directly to Siheung. Slaughter and Falge went to Musan-ni where Slaughter's dog, Jet, the first out of his kennel, went ballistic. His vicious barking unnerved his handler. Slaughter shouted at him, "Shut up, Jet! Ain't nobody out there!"

Later the men would move around among the four locations, but their dogs always went with them. All the areas the men and dogs would patrol were within fifty miles of the Thirty-Eighth Parallel, and all had huge ammunition storage facilities to be protected. It was getting cold in Korea by the time the men moved in, and it would only get colder. In the winter of 1954–1955, the weather was comparable to the frigid days at Chosin Reservoir in 1950. The men saw signs of the pending freeze as they drove to their posts. Koreans along the road were already picking up any scrap they could find to burn, and many tagged along behind the trucks as they went, hoping for coal or fuel to fall along the wayside. The poverty was striking, but the men were most concerned about what it would mean to care for the dogs in these conditions.

7

THE MISSION

The dogs were set up immediately in the kennels on the perimeter of the posts. The men found very little had been done to prepare for the dogs and the pending threat of winter worried them. The dogs' needs came first, always, and basic shelter had to be established. They also had concerns about the cans of horse meat freezing, so they set up potbelly stoves and burn barrels to keep the meat thawed.

At Yong Dong Po, where Harlan had left Greta only a few months before, there were still kennels from the group of 8125th who had gone before them, but the mission there was diminished and not the priority. The men never met Greta. No one even knew that she had been there. Perhaps she was moved to a different location along with the other dogs, but all the new group found were the vestiges of the former dog inhabitants.

In the other camps the men had to start from scratch. There had been no dogs in those places before them. It wasn't easy to scrape together spare lumber in Korea, because much of it had already been pilfered. They put in a request for supplies, but that would take months to receive—if the request was honored at all. So they set to work building the kennel areas using the same shipping crates that had carried the dogs from Carson. Those crates were very small, however, and the dogs wouldn't survive a Korean winter without some fortification. Some of the ammo storage units they had been sent to protect had remnants of wooden floors, and the men decided to use what they could of those. They set about building homes for the dogs and were willing to sacrifice their own supplies—and their own down time—to do it.

Other measures also had to be taken to keep the dogs warm. Some of the men put their own gloves on their dogs' paws to keep delicate pads from freezing. Occasionally, a dog might even be brought into

Warming horse meat on potbelly stoves was necessary in the frozen Korean wasteland.

The makeshift kennels were lovingly built to meet the dogs' every need.

the men's tent to keep it warm. Dogs' water would often be melted in helmets over the open fire pits.

Peterson and three of the other handlers in his section improvised on their bare bones conditions that winter by bringing the dogs into their tent. The already small space was consumed by four additional furry occupants who were almost as large as the men. The shared body heat was a bonus for both handlers and dogs. The situation was a definite detriment for anyone else who might try to enter the space, however. Once the Charge of Quarters (CQ) found this out when he entered the tent to wake them for their 11:00 p.m. shift. The dogs, though muzzled and chained, were startled by the intruder and tried to attack. The tent and its contents were destroyed, and the rattled CQ never went to their tent again. Instead, the next day a phone was installed in the tent.[1]

The Army wasted no time, regardless of the dogs' sleeping situation, in putting the dogs into rotation. The duty was a twelve-hour overnight shift, roughly from sunset to sunrise. They worked two days on and two days off in order to give the dogs necessary down time, which the Army realized was crucial to the dogs' well-being. Every morning on duty, the men would retrieve their dogs, check them thoroughly for any signs of injury or illness, slip on the choke chain, and grab their side arms. They patrolled the post perimeter and ammo areas throughout the night, looking for any signs of Koreans slipping past the boundaries. They had been taught to issue certain commands in Korean: "Halt," "Hands up," "Get on the ground," "Don't resist," and "stop struggling." The dog's primary job was to alert. Only as a last ditch effort, if the suspect did not respond to the litany of commands in Korean, were the soldiers to let a dog loose.

The dogs were so keenly aware of any sight, smell, or sound, that often they alerted to nothing. This made it difficult for the men, at first, to decipher what was really a threat. They were hyper-vigilant in the beginning. Once Stewart, already frightened from patrolling through a Korean cemetery, heard shooting in the distance. His instinct to "get down" kicked in, and he fell hard to the ground, closing his eyes to the imagined impact of a bullet on his body. When he opened his eyes, he looked to his side and found Duchess had also hit the deck. Slaughter's dog, Jet, had a reputation for being especially alert to any and all threats, perceived or real. After a while Slaughter caught on and could be heard patrolling through the night, saying, "Shut up, Jet! There's nobody out there!"

The men found over time that any suspects they encountered were generally completely submissive in the face of a dog. Because of this, the handlers could convince them to leave and never return. This was a huge relief for the men, who felt a deep compassion for what these civilians were enduring at home. Sometimes it was necessary to take civilians into custody, usually repeat offenders, but even Lieutenant Word's early promise of alcohol was not enough to override the compassion many felt for these Korean men trying to feed their starving families.

STARVATION

It was probably the scent of food coming from the active military posts that was most responsible for bringing hungry people to them. In the dead of winter, the men had to warm the dogs' food over the fire. Horse meat cooking over an open fire had a smell Fickes would later describe as "marvelous." Despite his American sensibilities, which could never quite accept the notion of horse as food for humans, he understood the draw—though he never sampled it.

Just as people were drawn to the smell, stray dogs who had managed to survive the Korean famine also could not resist the smell of the meat cooking. This brought the dogs to the posts, where some would make homes for as long as they were welcome. Only the true survivors lasted. The military working dogs were nasty about protecting their food. Schulz's dog had to be double-chained at feeding time, and Falge had developed a system of pulling his dog's empty pan away with a stick. Strays had to make buddies, either with one of the K-9s or with one of the soldiers.

There were set amounts of rations for dogs and people at the posts. Meat for the dogs and food for the soldiers were shipped through the quartermaster either from Japan or from the states. The men understood all too well that what was a single ration for them was more than the average Korean would eat in a week. The dogs often received more than they could eat, and leftover meat was to be discarded if it went past the expiration date, or if the dogs didn't eat their whole portion. Expiration dates and dog slobber were never a deterrent to the starving, however, and it was tough for the men to follow Army policy in the face of so much hunger. Often the Koreans would dig through the trash for the rotting meat. This was heart-breaking and difficult to watch, but it was also problematic to the mission. The men had tried taking the trash a greater distance from the posts, and they were always heartsick at having to pry the deter-mined Koreans from the truck's bumper. Finally, the Army set forth a policy that the Korean civilians were to stay out of the trash dump areas altogether because it only seemed to encourage them farther and farther inside the gates. Of course it was left to the dogs and handlers to enforce this policy that most did not condone.

At first the men tried to discourage the Koreans by putting Ex Lax on discarded horse meat. This was a last-ditch effort, and a hor-rific option: diarrhea could likely turn malnourishment into a death sentence. Still, they hoped one case of diarrhea would serve as suffi-cient warning for everyone else. They were wrong. So the men tried another tactic: knowing the fear and loathing the Koreans had for the dogs, the men put the dogs' feces, scooped up on a daily basis, on top of the discarded meat as the ultimate deterrent. This worked for a time, but it wasn't a huge leap for people already accustomed to knocking maggots off rotting food to look past dog feces for a meal.

The moral conflict the men felt was soul-crushing. They were bound by duty to make the dogs their first priority. They knew the dogs were well fed, usually with plenty left over at the end of the day to share. Yet military policy would not allow them to feed starving people. If one of them were to get caught allowing the Koreans to eat, he would be punished—some form of non-judicial punishment or even time in the brig. It was the latter option that most worried the men. To be sentenced to time in confinement would disrupt the handler-dog bond for an undetermined amount of time, and that defied the credo the dog handlers lived by. Dogs needed their handlers, and the handlers needed the dogs. A soldier would never abandon a fellow soldier on a mission.

Starving stray dogs, however, were another matter. The survivors managed to find a way into the tents of the men of the 8125th. There was no Army policy against feeding strays. This may have been because the Army had witnessed, throughout its illustrious history in war, that soldiers derived comfort from battle buddies. Perhaps it had more to do with keeping Korean combatants hungry by controlling a food source, the dogs. Whatever the reason, strays were left alone by military brass. The handlers, on the other hand, were drawn to any dog that wandered inside the perimeter. Maybe the dogs reminded them of the dogs they had known in their youth, or maybe it was the bond that they had formed with their K-9s. Once they endeared themselves, strays received full spoiling privileges. The men would never have taken scraps from their plates to their K-9 partners, but they happily gave food to the strays. Two of those strays, Katie and Posack, were even given the right to sleep at the foot of the bunk.

KATIE

When Benevenga first got to Siheung, he noticed a pair of hungry dogs hanging around the kennels. His initial thought was that they would certainly be attacked and killed by the K-9s if they ever got too close. From a distance, however, he could see that dog language flowed easily between the strays and the military working dogs, and there was never a problem. The two strays seemed to know which dogs they could befriend and which were off-limits. Chan's Prinz would stretch out to the end of his chain to meet the two dogs. Fickes's Duke was the same, and it was through him that any human was ever able to have contact with the pair.

Benevenga wanted desperately to get food to the stray dogs, but they were so mistrusting of humans that it made it difficult even to extend a bowl of food, much less a stroking hand. He left food for the pair when he could, and always found that the two had eaten in his absence. He hoped over time the dogs would allow for more. Once while out in the dog yard, Benevenga was surprised to find the stray dogs hadn't touched the bowl of food. His first terrible thought was that the Koreans had gotten to them. He had such an abiding love for dogs that this idea was beyond horrific. He tried to put it out of his mind as he completed his chores, tending to his dog's needs. Suddenly a noise caught his attention near Duke. The two dogs were playing with Duke. Benevenga walked up to them, hand extended, and to his surprise they paid him little mind. He got close enough to touch them and crouched down, cupping his hand as he extended it to their faces. The male stray recoiled a bit but didn't seem too fearful in Duke's presence. The female surprised Benevenga by fully surrendering to his touch.

"Hello there," he said smiling. "Do you need a name?" He decided to call her Katie—a beautiful girl's name, he thought. The male was decidedly more Korean, in appearance and demeanor, so he decided the more skittish dog would be called Posack.

That same night, Benevenga heard a scratching on the door to his tent. Katie, or "Kate" as Benevenga sometimes called her, had come to visit him. Surprising even himself, he opened the door to her and allowed her inside. She immediately went to his bunk, crawled underneath it, and fell fast asleep. Later that night she left a puddle in the middle of the living area, and Benevenga, suspicious of allowing dogs in the house anyway, gave her the boot out into the snow. She remained by his door for the rest of the night and followed him all the next day. The next night, as Benevenga went into the tent, dog and man exchanged glances—hers imploring, his skeptical. Benevenga relented. He opened the door to her and she returned to her spot under his bunk. From that day forward, she would cry to let him know she needed to be let out, and she never wet the floor again. After that, they were never separated. Posack, however, only let Ben get close from time to time, but never as close as Katie. She followed Benevenga everywhere he went, and he delighted in teaching her tricks. The men grew to know Katie and Benevenga as a team. Fickes got very close to Katie, too, because he and Benevenga were the best of friends.

Then, literally in a flash, everything changed.

One night Falge spilled a lot of fuel while he was trying to start a fire. Benevenga got accelerant on his arms, and when Falge struck the match, the whole front of his body went up in flames. Benevenga was tended to by the medics but was in critical condition. He would have to be transferred to the Army hospital in Japan for further treatment and would not be returning to his unit. He knew his military working dog, Gray, would be cared for, but he worried about Katie.

Fickes came to see him off from the medivac, and Benevenga asked for a promise. "Will you take care of Katie?"

Fickes wouldn't have had it any other way. "Bring her home if you can, Fickes." Benevenga knew that this was a promise Fickes might never be able to fulfill, but he wanted to put his dream out there and leave nothing behind.

"I'll take good care of her, Ben. Don't you ever worry."

Fickes completely fulfilled his promise to his friend. Katie became his constant companion. She slept under his bunk from then on and ate all his scraps. Fickes started taking Katie on patrol, off-leash, with him and Duke. She was a quick study and learned from Duke how to react to a threat. It was probably easier for her than it was for the highly trained K-9s to see the Koreans as threatening. She remembered a time when her life was in danger in their presence, and she acted accordingly. What she didn't pick up from Duke was equally beneficial. Duke was a bit of a scaredy cat, alerting to the regular creeping and groaning of a shifting building, growling at barrels of water, quivering over pheasants in the bushes. Maybe it was because Katie was more streetwise than Duke, but she seemed to have an innate understanding of which threats were real and which ones were only perceived.

Katie lived to protect Fickes, and before long he completely trusted his life with her. He even started taking Katie on patrol and leaving Duke behind. Duke didn't seem to mind; his heart had never been in it. Also, he still got all the attention, food, and exercise he had earned as a trained K-9. He was satisfied. Or maybe it was the satisfaction of

Fickes had plenty of K-9 assistance with his sentry duties.

his other urges that made him a bit lazy. Katie eventually had a puppy, and Fickes suspected it could have been Duke's offspring. He named the puppy Ben.

8

NEW BLOOD AND UNDYING LOYALTY

MELOCHICK

T he Korean Armistice, under the authority of the United Nations, was signed in July 1953, establishing the Demilitarized Zone along the Thirty-Eighth Parallel. In theory, this established a cease-fire between the two nations of North and South Korea. Yet the Americans' involvement in policing that action required the continued presence of ordnance handlers. Melochick and Simpson handled ordnance in the 696th in Uijongbu and the Fifty-Eighth Ordnance Company in Siheung. They were not there to hand out ordnance, but to sit on it in the event that uneasy tensions flared again.

Melochick had attended explosive ordnance disposal (EOD) school and thought he was going to Korea to handle explosives for soldiers in the field. When he arrived at the 696th Ordnance Company, Uijongbu (just twenty miles below the Thirty-Eighth Parallel), he was told that his services would be needed elsewhere. Guarding the ammunition, instead of handling it, had become the priority, and no one was more effective at that job than the 8125th Sentry Dog Detachment. He was going to "the Doggies."

As a brand new handler, Melochick was thrown into the quick course of dog-handling and was assigned Warrior, a huge, fierce dog. He felt rushed to "get in" on Warrior, and after taking him out for the first time got bitten. In what Melochick considered a stroke of luck, Warrior's sharp canines hit his watch. Melochick was certain his watch had saved his wrist from being broken.

Peterson reminded him, "Warrior trained at Carson and knows exactly what he's doing. He's just trying to see what he can get away with." The rookie was humbled—and a bit unnerved by his underestimation of Wolf's power.

Melochik was committed to making the best of his new situation. With persistence, and a few more close calls with Wolf, he became proficient and was assigned two more dogs. Each dog was a challenge in its own way, but he viewed their job as more art than mechanics and embraced the beauty of a dog's companionship. Dog handling, like explosives handling, could be exciting and dangerous, but the dogs had an irreplaceable quality that explosives lacked. Dogs were loyal, comforting, and even trustworthy. Regardless of Warrior's sometimes misplaced aggression, Melochick believed the dog would always protect him. Trust, an explicit quality in every man-dog relationship he encountered, was something he had never known in his family. Even the deep, trusting relationship between soldiers couldn't quite match the level of trust between man and dog. Melochick loved the feeling of harmonious synchronicity in dog handling, and he trusted his dogs with his life.

SIMPSON

Unlike Melochick, Simpson chose to be a dog handler. He had come to the Fifty-Eighth Ordnance Company at Siheung with a love of chemistry and a passion for the occupation he had learned in the Chem Corps. But there would be no active need for chemical, biological, or radiological specialists in that staging area of the Cold War. His education was shelved as he was asked to work CQ duty for the personnel at that post, including the men and dogs of the 8125th.

Simpson admired the guys in the 8125th. A dog lover from childhood, he also greatly admired the nobility of the K-9s. Chan and Prinz came into the CQ often, and he looked forward to those days. Prinz was easy to handle and loved to be scratched; Chan always made him laugh. He was able after a while to recognize most of the dogs at a glance. Some of his favorites were Wooden's dog, Chief, and the docile Blind Sam, always at Broadway's side. Having grown up on a farm with dogs, Simpson understood a little about the pack dynamic. Although he worried that the unit might be exclusive and unaccepting of outsiders without the same formal training, he asked Sergeant Nunn, a senior enlisted man who didn't have a dog but was over the unit's enlisted soldiers, about joining the team. To his surprise, Nunn told him that they could use all the help they could get. He believed Simpson was up for the challenge. In fact, he already had a dog in mind for Simpson.

Grey was one of the powerful dogs who had been difficult for most of the handlers so far. It was hard to get in on this aggressive dog, but Simpson, knowing the challenge ahead, made up his mind that he wouldn't fail. Grey's former handler had been injured while in Korea, leaving the K-9 without a dedicated teammate. Simpson had observed the interactions between Grey and his handler many times before his leaving, and had taken note of the quiet power with which the man addressed his dog. In spite of the dog's fierce demeanor, Simpson could decipher a lot from the way Grey held his ears, and by the low warbling tone of his guttural growl. Simpson let Nunn know that he was ready to start with Grey, and he formulated his approach.

He decided to go slowly into Grey's world and form a bond that would endure. It took several weeks with the bite suit and several more to practice tracking, but Grey was masterful at his job and guided his apprentice through his paces. Simpson had to learn to give commands, be a leader to his dog, and handle the dog with confidence in risky situations. Grey had to learn that Simpson was his new partner. It was an arduous process, but after many difficult days, and a consistent training regimen, Nunn came to Simpson and told him they were ready. He and Grey would be moved to Uijongbu where they would join Stewart and Duchess, Hatch and Willy, Melochick and Warrior, and many of the other teams who had by then become veterans of sentry work in Korea. Simpson looked forward to their sage advice. He admitted to them straight away, "The dog trained me."

VAL

Like the other men, Simpson was assigned a second dog to handle while in Korea. Val had all of the aggressive nature of Grey without any of the control. The men said Val was "crazy," and Simpson believed them. On his first encounter with Val, the beast bit Simpson and tore the flesh on his hand wide open. Still, Simpson would not give up. He believed they could make a partnership work.

He labored to find Val's soft spot, and when he did, tried to play to it whenever possible. It wasn't authorized, but Simpson learned from the others that Val loved to track rabbits. This was done off-leash, however, and if this violation was discovered, Simpson could be court-martialed for the unlawful use of a weapon. Yet Simpson knew this activity could only make Val a better, healthier dog all around. It was a risk he was willing to take for his partner.

Once, while enjoying his favorite pastime, Val caught a rabbit's scent and stopped dead in his tracks. Simpson looked down at Val's feet and saw a tripwire which, as he traced its origin, he found attached to a Bouncing Betty explosive device. In his time with EOD he had learned how to defuse these ordnance, and he did so, quickly and quietly. He praised Val for saving his life knowing that he would have hit the tripwire, right in his path, if Val had not alerted first. In fact, if Val had not stopped right at that spot, the dog would have been blown to pieces, too. No one ever found out about the tripwire; he told himself it was a secret he would carry to his grave.

Simpson never managed to form a deep bond with Val, at least not the kind he had with Grey. Simpson understood Val for what he was: a weapon with a heartbeat. He needed care, the same level of care and compassion that all living beings need, but no one could ever let their guard down around him. Val had proven over and over that he would turn and strike without notice, making him dangerous to both friend and foe. The only thing Simpson could hope for with Val was a mutual understanding. To reach that understanding, Simpson resorted to using a controversial technique.

The "helicopter roll" was a technique the handlers were taught at Carson to bring an enraged dog under control. As the name implies, the handler would grab a charging dog's leash and swing the dog by the collar, like a helicopter blade, before slamming the dog to the ground. This was a last-ditch effort for desperate handlers. It had been ingrained in them that the dogs were never to be physically punished. If a soldier was caught even lightly striking a dog, he would be charged with destruction of government property and receive severe punishment, ranging from judicial (with time served in the brig) to non-judicial (being separated from the unit or even the Army with a "Less Than Honorable" discharge). This technique was only to be used when a handler's life was threatened. The method most often knocked the dog unconscious without killing it, obviously preferable to pulling out a firearm and shooting the dog. Still, deciding whether to perform the helicopter roll was never easy.

Stewart had to use the technique on Spooks, the dog he started handling in Korea after Duchess went "tame." "Tame" was a term the men used to describe a dog who had made it through training but failed to have the heart for attack in country. This was a good description for Duchess, except that it didn't take into consideration that she was probably tame—a pet—before she ever came to the Army. Spooks, however, had been known for his ferocity, and Stewart felt safer with him while on patrol.

The helicopter roll came about out of pure adrenaline on Stewart's part. Spooks had gotten in a fight with another dog when he suddenly turned his focus on Stewart and attacked him from the back. In the scuffle Spooks gained a strong hold on Stewart's leg. As Stewart spun around attempting to separate Spook's fangs from his thigh, he also instinctually lifted him off the ground, spinning and then bringing him hard to the ground again. Spooks was disoriented. Coming to, the K-9 shook his head and sat looking at Stewart as if nothing had ever happened. The technique had accomplished what Stewart needed at the time, but Spooks never really recovered. He remained mistrustful of Stewart for the rest of their time together, but he never attacked him again. Stewart couldn't say that he ever completely trusted Spooks again, either.

Simpson, like most of the men, was conflicted about the technique because he had taught the dog to attack him and encouraged raw aggression. He understood that it could be confusing for some dogs to know when attacking was right, since furious behavior was always rewarded. Yet when Val barreled down on him one day, teeth gnashing at his flesh midair, Simpson didn't stop to think. He reacted with force by instinct. Val was a little loopy after being flung to the ground, and Simpson used the opportunity to subdue the dog and muzzle him. The show of force worked. Val had a newfound respect for Simpson, and from that time on the two worked together well. Val was able to compartmentalize the experience and quickly adapt to his new reality: Simpson was the boss, not the enemy. Regardless of Val's changed behavior, Simpson was never able to think of him as anything other than a mean dog again.

Val and Spooks had survival instincts which drove them to see humans in general as a threat to life. Granted, it was humans who had taught them this lesson and betrayed their trust by not understanding how deep a dog's instinct could go. The handlers had a constant kinship with their dogs, and this level of intimacy let them know the dogs in their unit who would cross the line between loyalty and madness. Regardless, Army policy always trumped individual experience. There was no way to separate the dogs who had been driven mad from the ones who would become maddened by their protectiveness of the handler. Dogs like Val and Spooks were used in the rotation even at the risk of the handler's safety. So the men, like Simpson and Stewart, had to work with what they had in each dog while hoping for the best.

CHIEF

Chief was one of the dogs whose loyalty bound him to his handler, and he willingly did what was asked of him—even to death. The men agreed that Chief could be a tough dog. He was driven and focused, especially when it came to the pursuit of a fleeing suspect. He could be showy in his aggression, a necessary characteristic for keeping desperate and threatened suspects from resorting to outright violence.

One night while on duty, Chief's handler, Wooden, released him to pursue an intruder. Off-leash, he got beyond his handler's sight. When Wooden heard a yelp, he thought Chief must have made contact with the fleeing man. Then there was brief whimpering, followed by silence. Wooden's heart and mind began to race, and the stillness became deafening. He hastened to find his dog, wondering if Chief had caught the intruder—or if the intruder had harmed the dog. Approaching a barbed wire fence on the perimeter, Wooden's heart dropped. Chief had been caught on the fence by his collar and hanged himself. The gruesome scene wrenched Wooden's gut and broke his heart. He had seen animals wounded and injured many times before, having worked on California racetracks before joining the Army. He had even had to put down horses himself. But Chief had been his closest ally. He lost one of his best friends that day. When Wooden returned to camp with Chief in his arms, the group of boisterous men fell silent, too. One of their own had been lost, and many bowed their heads in sadness. Simpson helped Wooden with Chief's body and started making preparations for an immediate burial.

Simpson dug the grave in an old Korean cemetery just outside the post. The men and their dogs gathered around the burial site and watched as Chief was laid in the ground. His collar and leash, the placard with his serial number, and his muzzle went into the ground with him. The men cried openly over the dog's still body and laid flowers on his burial mound. They placed a stone where his head rested and talked about how they would have it engraved later with his name and death date so that no one would ever forget him and his service to the United States Army and to his handler, Wooden. Some Korean civilians looked on as they buried Chief, curious but reverent.

The next day, Simpson went out to check on Chief. From a distance he could see that the grave had been disturbed, and he started to boil with rage. When he reached the site, he became ill. The mementoes of Chief's life remained in the barren hole, but Chief's body had been taken. For the first time, the horrors of Korea hit him with full force. He hated it there and wanted to go home. He thought about Grey and was comforted to think that he would be brought back to Camp Carson when it was all over. He started to cry as he prepared to return to Wooden and the other men with the horrible message: Chief would never be at rest.

9

BLIND SAM

To Chan's surprise, his correspondence with Mary Jay continued. He had thought her interest might wane because he had so little to tell about Prinz. Other than the daily routine, there wasn't much to share. He couldn't tell her that "patrol," for Prinz, meant a walk to the chow hall or a stroll to CQ. Apparently the relative lack of information didn't matter. In her last letter she had told Chan, "I think I might be in love with you." He felt sure that she wouldn't probe for much detail on Prinz's actual role as a war dog.

Chan felt a little guilty about leaving Prinz out of the rotation. He was allowed to choose any of the dogs, and he felt safer with a more ferocious protector—but at least he knew Prinz was okay and his needs were met. Prinz always looked a little forlorn when he went back to the kennel, but Chan rationalized that it was best for both of them. Prinz couldn't protect him the way King could, and Chan even wondered if the dog would protect himself if push ever came to shove. Besides, Prinz wasn't the only dog who didn't "work" for his supper. Several of the dogs had, no doubt, come from similar backgrounds and didn't really have the heart for sentry work.

Other dogs were not healthy enough to patrol. Sam, Prinz's kennel neighbor, was one of those dogs. He had become blind while in Korea due to a degenerative disease that progressed with age. Cataracts had clouded his eyes in Korea, making him appear older than he really was, and his vision was almost non-existent. All of the handlers had become worried for his safety in the field. Old Blind Sam (as Broadway called him in his languid Texas drawl) had the sweetness of a dog who had lived a long life close to loving humans. But he wasn't as old as his appearance would make anyone believe. Although they had no background on him (he had been in Korea since 1953 and had gone through Camp Carson long before this group of handlers), the men believed him to be middle-aged, roughly five or six years old. When his vision failed, he was taken out of rotation and put in an area of the kennel set aside for the sick, the old, and the docile dogs of the 8125th. There he would rendezvous with Prinz.

Prinz and Sam ate their meals together sometimes, and took naps in the sun when it dared to show its face in the Korean sky. Prinz felt at ease in Sam's presence. Spending time with Sam also meant Prinz saw Chan more often. Broadway and Chan were good friends, and Broadway spent a lot of time with Sam. Prinz missed the constant contact with Chan that he had had back home in Colorado, and he lived for the moments when he was by his side. Often, Blind Sam and Prinz would stroll the base together with Chan and Broadway. Prinz would guide his canine friend with his own body away from things he was sure Sam could no longer sense. It was in those moments that his life felt like the old one he had left behind in Maine, and he was happy.

Broadway also loved being around Sam, and eventually he let the dog tag along with him nearly everywhere he went. Sam went with Broadway to the Post Exchange, the barber shop, the chow hall, and CQ to do necessary paperwork. Sometimes at CQ Sam would sit at Simpson's feet—before Simpson moved over to Uijongbu—and wait for Broadway to finish his chores. Sam loved when snacks would magically appear in Simpson's hand, and he was content to sit there for hours on the slightest possibility that they might.

IN THE LINE OF DUTY

Broadway still had sentry work to do, and for that he needed more than a companion—Sam couldn't follow him on duty. The shifts for handlers were from sundown to sunup, usually four nights on and three nights off in a week. Broadway and his working dog, Rex, were given the dreaded task of guarding the farthest perimeter of the post in complete darkness, often in frigid temperatures. He was always glad to have Rex by his side on those long nights, knowing that he was the most effective weapon in the arsenal. All the handlers agreed that just having that weapon brought peace of mind. Moreover, the handlers had no question that their weapon was precise and deadly. However, Broadway continued to hope that he would never have to unleash it.

One night while they were guarding the perimeter, Rex alerted with a low growl. This wasn't unusual in the sentries. Trained for sensitivity to any possible threat, they would grumble and bark at all kinds of noises in the night. This time, however, Rex was different. The hackles on Rex's back raised, mirroring the hair that lifted on

Broadway's arm. Rex threw his head low, and Broadway crouched beside him. The two moved together toward the threat, suspended in an eerie quiet. Rex wasn't barking yet, and Broadway listened with intensity. The threat was coming toward them. Before flicking on his flashlight, he called "halt" in Korean.

The beam of light found the Korean man, a civilian, well inside the perimeter, moving toward them, his posture aggressive. He might have had something in his hand, but Broadway couldn't tell whether or not it was a weapon. Broadway called out to him a few more times, almost pleading for him to stop. The man barreled forward and seemed to be looking at the dog. Broadway could feel Rex quivering in anticipation all the way through the leash. He knew Rex was waiting for the order to do what he had been trained to do. Broadway hesitated, called out one last time to the intruder who ignored him, then dropped the leash. "Get him!"

Rex was a rocket, and he took the man down like a lion on its prey. Broadway could see that Rex had gone for the face and throat, an area that all the dogs had learned in bite training was unprotected and vulnerable. He waited to call the dog off because he didn't know if there was a weapon involved. Broadway was just as much concerned for Rex as his own safety, and he wanted his dog to be able to protect himself. Thankfully, Rex seemed to have the upper hand. As he got closer to the scene he could see that the man was struggling. Rex had been taught to keep pressure while the perpetrator resisted. The more the man struggled, the more Rex sank in, shaking the man and writhing on top of him to maintain his grip. Broadway repeatedly told the man to stop resisting, but the man kept screaming and trying to get away.

Finally, Broadway had to pull Rex off. They struggled awhile before he was able to get a muzzle on him and contain him. The intruder lay on the ground, bleeding from deep oozing punctures all over his body. His eye was so mangled that Broadway was unsure if it still remained in its socket. It was the gushing femoral artery which concerned him most. He applied pressure, but he needed assistance immediately to keep the man alive. Broadway pulled out his pistol and fired a series of three shots, the unit's signal for help. He waited, not knowing if he had been heard, then repeated the chain again.

It was more than an hour before help arrived. He stayed by the man's side throughout, checking vitals and trying to keep him conscious. In their time together, only able to communicate a few words in Korean, he tried to keep the man positive and hopeful. He ascertained that the man did not have a weapon. Maybe he had and dropped it. His fellow handlers arrived on the scene and congratulated him and Rex. The dog, knowing he had done a good job, wagged his tail and soaked in the praise. Broadway was much less cheerful. He realized that if the man died, he would have to live with a mixed sense of guilt over taking a life. Above all else, though, he was grateful to Rex for saving them from what he still believed had been a life-threatening situation.

The Korean man was rushed to the big hospital in Seoul. Medics worked on him in transport, as he slipped in and out of consciousness. He was stabilized at the hospital for a while, but two days after the attack, he died from his injuries. Rex became the only dog of the 8125th ever attributed with a kill.

HEALING WORK

Broadway continued working with Rex. Patrols were uneventful, and the two went about business as usual. Overall, Broadway was satisfied with his work. Then an opportunity arose for him to take on the role of a vet-tech. To his own surprise, he was open to it.

The vet-techs were not trained as such. They were handlers who took on the responsibility of all the medical care for the dogs in the absence of a veterinarian. Broadway's friend Heiney (just a grumpy kid who hated the Army and acted like an 80-year-old man, Broadway joked) had been the unit's vet-tech, but he had moved on to another job and left the position open. All the handlers at Camp Carson had learned basic canine first aid and care. They could also humanely put a dog down if necessary and certify their death certificates for Army purposes. Broadway considered the position carefully, knowing he would have to stop working with Rex on a daily basis. Rex knew his feelings on a level he believed the dog never could for anyone else. But Broadway also loved the dogs, like Blind Sam, who needed someone to care for them. Then he remembered that the vet-techs didn't have night patrols. It was the idea of a regular full night's sleep that sold him.

It was good for Broadway's soul to take a step back from nightly patrols. He found a peace in caring for the dogs, and he got to spend more time with Blind Sam. Through his new job, he made a lot of connections with the Korean community as well. On the sly, he began giving horse meat to a missionary who ran an orphanage for Korean children, most of them left parentless and starving by the war. Broadway was stealing from the government to do this, but he didn't care about the consequences. He knew, maybe for the first time since arriving in Korea, that he was doing the right thing. Over time, the relationship between Broadway and the missionary became a true friendship.

Broadway would deliver the meat to the orphans as often as he could without getting caught, and to the delight of the children he brought Sam along. Maybe because the missionary himself had such a deep love for Sam, the children trusted him. They would flock around him when he came, petting and hugging him. Sam loved their attention. This, Broadway was convinced, was Sam's true mission in Korea. He was never meant to be hardened; he was meant to be a dog.

10

DOWN TIME

The patrols in Korea were long and rough for both the men and the dogs. They battled the elements together, especially the bitter cold. The equipment they had been issued was not sufficient to protect them from the winter weather. So-called "Mickey Mouse" boots—thermal insulated boots, named after the beloved cartoon character because they were so big—and parkas were at a premium because of their usefulness. For the most part their uniforms were hand-me-downs from the World War II era, and their tents were the same. Each tent was outfitted with a potbellied stove, but wood was a scarcity. The men felt they would never be able to make a fire hot enough to keep the arctic air at bay. If the dogs could talk, they might have had the same complaint. Their kennels weren't insulated against the winter wind, which was sharp enough to cut through the dogs' lush coats. On patrol, the men would often keep their bodies as close as possible to the dogs for shared body heat. At least the dogs' meals were always warm, because the horse meat would freeze in the can and had to be thawed on an open fire. Many of the handlers, lured by the idea of a hot meal, would sample the horse meat before giving it to the dogs.

The summer months brought discomfort to a whole new level. It could get very hot in the middle of Korea, with swarms of tormenting bugs and very little shade to escape. Worms and mange were huge problems for the dogs in that climate, and they required regular worming and baths. On patrols the men would carry extra canteens for the dogs. The physicality of the dogs' work demanded three times the water in hot weather to keep them hydrated, and their heavy fur coats only exacerbated the problem. Luckily for the teams at Uijongbu, there was a river flowing near their post. The men would often, in their downtime, grab their dogs and head to the river to cool off. They

The dogs loved a swim in the river as much as the men, or maybe more so.

used that opportunity to give the dogs their antiseptic baths and have fun. On the hottest days the river would be dotted with GIs in their skivvies, floating in the cool stream with a swimming dog at the end of a leash, pulling them along.

It was important, especially in the hazardous line of work of the 8125th, to have sufficient time to unwind. The Army recognized that and afforded the men those occasions. But Army policy only allowed for dogs to be given time off the rotation in order to heal and recuperate, not for recreation. This meant that after regulation grooming or being checked over and treated by their handlers or vet-techs, the dogs were left chained to a stake near their kennels. The handlers recognized their dogs' need for play and socialization, however, even if they had to be muzzled in the process. So the men took the dogs with them wherever they could. This was especially true when the men went hiking, a favorite pastime for many of them. The dogs weren't authorized to be off-leash on these outings, but the men knew their dogs and took the necessary precautions to keep people safe while still allowing the dogs some much needed exercise. The handlers were willing to accept the consequences if they got caught, because they saw the benefit for everyone if the dogs were physically and mentally sound and balanced.

Lieutenant Word and Sergeant Fowler (he had become sergeant in Korea) were two of the leaders who, because of their intimacy with the men and dogs of the 8125th, knew that letting the dogs run was crucial. Although they didn't have dedicated dogs themselves, they took the time to give dogs recreation in their down time. The two men had hunted from childhood, and they endeavored to continue that activity in Korea. When they had the time, they would find an off-duty dog and take it into the countryside to help them in the hunt. The Shepherds, with their strong prey drive, could easily be trained to hunt down rabbit. Some of the more docile dogs still retained a soft palate and were able to retrieve ducks and geese for the men. After a while they had some favorite dogs and were always disappointed when these K-9s were on duty and couldn't go with them.

Occasionally the men were offered rest and relaxation time, and they would take the time to get off the post and see Korea. Simpson and Stewart took R&R together once and went into Seoul. They marveled at the craftsmanship and artistry of the Korean city. More profoundly, they realized that people were starving in the big cities just as much as they were in the small villages. On that trip, the two

Fickes brings a runner home and helps the 8125th to victory.

men gave children money whenever they could. Simpson found it painful at times because there was never enough to care for them all.

Overall, the men made the best of their leisure hours and found things to do even when they had to create them. Chan formed a baseball league on post and got other units to play the 8125th in regular games. They had two winning seasons while in Korea. Fickes bought a ukulele and learned to play the entire Burl Ives songbook. There was always someone up for a game of cards. Many of the guys had cameras and took up photography.

Hatch and Simpson regularly photographed Korean cemeteries because the stacked stones and remnants of ancestors' lives made them visually interesting subjects. Once they took a hike together in the mountains and found a Korean monastery where they sat for a little while with the monks.

Sometimes the boys just had to be boys.

Falge and some of the other guys fashioned a horseshoe pit. Chan taught Bakken how to play chess, and even when Chan took his queen off the board, no one could beat him. Jellison and Talley, both married men, preferred to hang out together and away from any shenanigans. They went to the exchange a lot and patronized local craftsmen who came there to make good money. Once, Jellison brought his dog Tex in to sit for a portrait painted by one of the artists.

All the guys agreed that their best time off was when Debbie Reynolds came with the USO. Some of the guys and dogs had to work security for the event, but they didn't mind. Security only got them closer to the starlet.

Of course, not all ways of passing the time were wholesome or beneficial. Drinking was a way to while away the hours of loneliness and boredom, and many of the guys partook. One of the men, Mardunkle, was prone to drinking to excess. Once he was standing out-

Hanging at the Enlisted Club with local girls was a welcome distraction.

side the Enlisted club, very drunk, his dog Cheetah at his side. Someone walked by and made a comment about Cheetah. Mardunkle flew into a rage and tried to beat the man to death with his bare hands. One of the other handlers had to grab Cheetah, who had also become enraged, and move him away from the scene to protect everyone.

The men of the 8125th had been issued ammunition, but they used very little of it, usually choosing their dog weapons instead. Since they were stationed at facilities that stored ammo, however, the men would burn powder whenever they could. Many hours were spent shooting at targets both authorized and unauthorized. Sometimes drinking would go hand-in-hand with the shooting, and many close calls and near misses—too many to count—were born from this hazardous combination.

Inevitably, there were girls around the alcohol, too. Fickes once marveled at Chan because he seemed to be constantly rejecting the advances of Korean girls. He told the other guys, "Chin needs a dog to protect him from all the girls chasing him." Prostitutes abounded around the camp, and Chan caused a great deal of embarrassment for one when she realized his name was her family's name, too.

It was difficult to stay out of trouble for many of the young men so far from home. Most managed to keep the shenanigans to a minimum and avoid punishment. A few were not so lucky. Fickes went to the stockade once for dereliction of duty. Bakken got into some trouble over an incident in town where he was accused of using his dog, Bullett, to threaten the mayor. He received counseling for the event but was able to prove that it mostly wasn't true. Sometimes the dogs were used in the troublemaking. Once while on patrol, Hatch found a Jeep parked on a dark back road on post. The doors of the Jeep were open, and he could see inside where a lieutenant and young nurse were kissing. He alerted his dog, Willy, to the "suspects" and released him on the lovers. Hatch knew full well that Willy was hard to pull off anyone (he couldn't get him off Chan once, because Willy mistook him for a Korean), so it was almost miraculous that the couple managed to keep the dog from tearing them apart. Furious, the lieutenant threatened Hatch's career, but to tell the story would have forced him to admit that he and the nurse were in an unauthorized area, doing unauthorized things. Hatch never received official punishment.

Garfield absolutely hated the Army, his job, and Korea. In general, he never wanted to be a dog handler, although he made it through training and had a decent connection with his dog. He might have resented the fact that he was thrown into dog handling without a choice, or maybe he just despised authority, but Korea—the smells, the distance, the life—sent him careening into despair and alcoholism. Many of his fellow handlers thought he just had an inferiority complex and wanted the world to think of him as "a badass." Initially he tried to stay out of trouble, especially by keeping busy. Often, he would ask Broadway if he could take his shifts. Broadway gave him a few, but ultimately, it wasn't enough to keep him out of trouble.

No one knows if Garfield chose to appear insane (so that he might get a discharge from the Army), or if he was truly imbalanced. His first attempt at getting out of Korea was running away. He walked about ten miles down a set of railroad tracks, towards Seoul, before he got picked up. He was charged with dereliction of duty and put on cleaning detail. Next, he shot himself in the leg. The bullet grazed him, leaving only a minor flesh wound. Maybe he thought if he could get a stay in the psych ward, the Army would grant him a discharge on the grounds of insanity. Instead they treated the wound and let him go back to work.

As time went on, Garfield began drinking more and more. He started drinking on the job as well as in his off hours. One night Garfield went out drunk, pulled out his pistol, and shot up a nearby Korean home. No one was injured, but this act landed him in the stockade for a long time. When he was finally released, he was branded with a "P" on the back of his uniform to mark him as a prisoner. He still was not discharged.

In his last act of hostility against the powers-that-be, Garfield stole a hand grenade. He asked his fellow soldiers, "I wonder what will happen if I throw this in the latrine?" Then he walked into the latrine, pulled the pin, threw the grenade down the hole, ran out the door, and waited about five seconds. There was an explosion, followed by copious amounts of feces raining from the sky. Garfield was immediately thrown back into the stockade where he remained until the end of the 8125th's deployment. He did eventually receive a dishonorable discharge, but he didn't get to leave Korea early as he had hoped.

Korea could be a devastating place for the heart and soul. But as is the true nature of heroes, the men, for the most part, found a way to rise above it all. No matter what the day's troubles held, devastating or disheartening, the men knew they always had each other. No one was allowed to sit and wallow. If one man saw another man in distress, he would go to him and make him laugh. The jokes could be downright raunchy, or they could be as pristine as an old-fashioned gag. Whatever it took to get them back on track, they would do for one another, and laughter was their go-to balm for almost everything that ailed them.

The dogs, too, proved time and again that they had magical healing powers of their own. It wasn't uncommon for the men, when life got too rough or homesickness set in, to go to the kennels and "play."

Just a game of fetch, or even a long walk off-leash, could soothe a tired soldier's mind. These were times that reminded a man of home, family, or a farm dog at his side. It gave a crazy existence a sense of normalcy once again. And the simple act of grooming, a job requirement that no man minded, slowed racing hearts and brought peace to their souls. The dogs never refused the attention and their loyalty was their gift.

11

THE
DEMONSTRATIONS

I n the summer of 1955, the men and dogs of the 8125th had hit
their stride. They had been guarding perimeters for nine months
and were coming to the end of their deployment. Starting in
1954 and continuing through that same summer, South Korea
erupted with violent protests throughout the country. Having
survived the war and resulting starvation, the people were desperate for the autonomy from the North that they had been promised
in the armistice. United Nations inspectors were in the country
under the banner of ensuring that freedom. Many of the South
Korean people, however, were reluctant to believe that inspectors
from Poland and the Czech Republic were at all neutral. The South
Koreans feared that they were spies for the North in the country
to perpetuate communist ideology. Massive and violent riots
sprang up as a result, and many times American soldiers, policing

for the United Nations and guarding United States interests, became the target of group attacks. South Korean President Syngman Rhee disavowed the violence, but it only escalated the mistrust of the populace.[1]

The men and dogs of the 8125th had no way of knowing that their mission was about to take a drastic turn. Orders came down for two of the four groups of the 8125th to go to Wolmido Island that summer for riot control. The Army had been turning fire hoses and tear gas on the people whenever necessary to thwart the attacking Koreans, but these methods had been ineffectual. United Nations offices had been penetrated, and at least forty-four Americans had been injured in the attacks. The Army recognized that the dogs remained one of the best kept secrets in Korea. The people were terrified of them, and military officials knew that they were the most effective weapon for keeping angry Korean mobs under control. It was largely a psychological weapon, but one the Army knew would work with very little collateral damage.

Chan and Broadway were called to take King and Rex to Osan and Wolmido Island for riot control. Chan had always feared that he might have to take someone's life, and now it looked as if he might see his fears realized. The throngs of people crashed gates and threw whatever they could grab at American soldiers. The dogs were in a frenzy with people and noises coming at them from every direction. Yet that frenzy turned out to be their salvation. No dogs were released during the riots, but their fury created a solid line the rioters never dared cross. Chan understood in those moments how invaluable the dogs were in the Korean mission. It was also increasingly clear that the Koreans would never be able to trust the dogs, and at least some of the dogs would never make peace with the Koreans.

Paulus had something special with Fritz from the very beginning at Carson. On seeing his dog for the first time, Paulus thought he was beautiful and felt an instant pride in him. He got in on Fritz quicker than most. There seemed to be an instant understanding between them. This is not to say that Fritz didn't challenge Paulus. Paulus could be heard mumbling to Fritz in those early days, "You are one stubborn dog." Fritz even tried to bite Paulus at first, but the handler believed in his dog and understood to play to Fritz's natural curiosity. Paulus knew his dog was smart, even smarter than most. Before long, Fritz had surpassed what was asked of him in training, and he became a standout in the sea of snarling dogs.

In Korea, Paulus and Fritz worked patrol in the first months. Fritz proved on those long patrols that he was more than capable of the

Paulus and Fritz stand ready.

work. He could be trusted to work off-leash, and his recall was excellent. Paulus had no doubt that Fritz would hear and obey his commands in an instant, and the unit's officers and NCOs took note of that. It was rare for this rag-tag group of dogs to be so consistent in obedience. This was not due to an inconsistency in training, but to the differences in their ages and upbringing prior to their military service. Few dogs were as pliable as Fritz. Only one other matched him, and that was Poole's dog, Rin-Tin.

Paulus and Poole were approached by their leaders in 1955, around the same time the riots were occurring in Korea. The Army wanted to form a demonstration team with their dogs, as they began to outline a different approach for the dogs. Until now the dogs had been used in psychological warfare against the Korean people, especially during the riots. Now the Army hoped to prove they could also be an aid to these same people. The Republic of Korea Army, a U.S. ally, had also witnessed the power and seeming savagery of the dogs. They believed the dogs had been trained to hate Korean people, not just anyone who threatened their handlers. The United States Army now hoped to convince ROK generals that the dogs could be their allies as well.

Paulus and Poole both agreed to make up this demo team with their superstar dogs, Fritz and Rin-Tin. At this time, Paulus still believed most of the dogs with the 8125th could be retrained and desensitized to transition back into civilian homes. Of course, they could prove to the ROK Army that the dogs could transition in another military's working dog program with ease. But Paulus wondered why the U.S. Army cared about the ROK Army starting a military working dog program of its own. Perhaps they wanted to illustrate the effectiveness of K-9s in crowd control and protection so that when the 8125th took its dogs home, their allies wouldn't require their services any longer. This theory fit with the news they had been learning from back home. The 8125th at Carson, although not yet decommissioned, had not sent any new handlers or dogs through training. The scouts remained active at Camp Carson, but scouts weren't needed in Korea. Only sentries could do the detail that had been done in the Cold War country. Paulus rested in those thoughts and committed to doing the best job he could do in convincing the Koreans that the dogs were the most effective weapon a sentry could possess.

In their demonstrations, they would first illustrate the sheer power sentry dogs possessed. Paulus and Poole would take turns putting on the bite suit and fleeing from their pursuing dogs. Of course, this wasn't necessary to prove the point to the ROK generals; the dogs' reputations for attack had preceded them. It was the second step which made the point they hoped to drive home. After illustrating what the dogs could do, Paulus and Poole would show the amount of control handlers had over the dogs. Paulus had trained Fritz to stop whatever he was doing on command.

During the demonstrations, the handlers would call a VIP from the stands, usually one of the general's liaisons, and ask him to flee from the dogs without the bite suit on. This would require immense courage on the part of the "perpetrator," but since they were unwilling to appear weak in front of their allies, the ROK soldiers accepted the challenge time and again. The man would run while Fritz remained in a stay at Paulus's heel. Only when Paulus made a hand gesture and ordered, "Get him," would Fritz take off, hyper-focused on apprehending the perpetrator. When Fritz reached the point of jumping for the jugular, Paulus would call out to him, "Stop!" Fritz would freeze in midair, turn, and run back to his handler. This move always elicited an audible gasp from the audience and let the handlers know they had done their job.

Paulus and Poole were proud of their dogs. They seemed to illustrate the very best qualities of all K-9s and the potential for learning new tricks each one possessed. At the end of every demonstration, the crowd was invited to have a meet-and-greet with the handlers and dogs. Paulus and Poole loved showing off the dogs. The men hoped to illustrate in those close and personal moments the specialness of the bond between dog and handler. They wanted the ROK soldiers to grasp the supreme level of loyalty and trust, companionship and care, that could exist between them and a military working dog. Paulus believed if they could connect with the dog, look into the dog's eyes, the soldiers would be sold. Unfortunately, it quickly became apparent the ROK soldiers were not making the connections they had hoped for. When Paulus invited them to pet Fritz, most would visibly recoil.

Paulus and Poole continued the demo team for many months, preaching their message whenever and wherever they had an audience. The men knew they couldn't afford to fail this mission. They would be going home to Camp Carson in a few short months, and the dogs would be going with them.

As it turned out, the demo team had brought more interest to the work of the 8125th than anyone had anticipated. For the first time since their arrival in Korea, the men started to encounter ROK officers on random and unscheduled occasions at the kennels. Simpson had one of the more dramatic encounters while working alone with Grey. He heard a helicopter coming in for a landing. When it landed, a three-star Korean general stepped out without an official U.S. government escort. Simpson almost went into panic mode. Grey sensed it and started to bark and spin in excited anticipation.

Simpson had learned enough Korean in his time there to get by in casual conversation. The general, seeing him with the dog, walked up to him and immediately began asking questions. From these questions, Simpson gleaned that his interest was in Grey. Simpson could tell that the officer wanted a demonstration of Grey's prowess, so he tried to give him what he requested.

In broken Korean, Simpson asked the general to sit and invited him to watch. He knew he wasn't authorized to demonstrate bite techniques, but he felt it would be harmless to show some basic obedience tricks. He had learned the obedience commands in Korean but Grey had not. He decided to wing it. In Korean, Simpson told Grey to sit. Grey sat, not because he understood the word but because of the corresponding hand gesture. The general's interest was piqued. "Down," Simpson ordered Grey in Korean, swooping his palm downward. Grey went into a down. "Good boy," he told Grey in Korean. Grey wagged his tail, understanding the universal language of approval between men and dogs in their mutual gaze. Simpson continued to send Grey out and to ask him to come. As a final act he asked Grey to "roll over" in Korean. Simpson could see out of the corner of his eye the delight in the general's face. The general stood up, uttered a thanks in Korean, walked back to the helicopter, and flew away. Simpson thought it an odd encounter and put it out of his mind.

A few days after the unauthorized demonstration, Simpson was called into Lieutenant Word's office. He knew that this had something to do with the general, and he expected some fallout from his violation. But when he walked in and reported, he was stunned to see a smile spreading across the lieutenant's face. After the demonstration, the general had been so impressed with Grey that he immediately requested all the dogs to be sent over to ROK training. He wanted all of them for his own military working dog kennel. Simpson's heart sank. Those dogs were theirs, heart and soul, and the idea of giving them over to anyone else was absurd.

Lieutenant Word's nonchalance on the matter perturbed Simpson, but he managed to ask respectfully what his response to the general had been. Word smiled. "I told him hell, no! Those are the finest dogs in the world and they are property of the U.S. Army."

Simpson's initial relief began to fade as he walked away from the office. He pondered all the pieces of the puzzle only to reach a bitter conclusion: there was no way the insistent Korean general would let this rest on a lieutenant's word. He tried hard to put it out of his mind before returning to his dog. If he returned to Grey with this negative energy, the K-9 would sense it and their day wouldn't go well. He did hug Grey when he got to the kennels, however, soothing his troubled spirit and congratulating the dog on a job well done.

12

SHORT TIMERS

The days for the men and dogs of the 8125th were rapidly drawing to a close. Not a single man among them could say he was sad about leaving Korea. Everyone was homesick and longing for a place where peace and rest were more prevalent than chaos and despair. They had been cold, colder than they had ever known. They had endured exhaustion and fear on long and fretful nights of patrol. The extraordinary poverty and despair of the people around them troubled them to the core. It enraged many of the handlers who had been asked to meet that desperation with violence when they really wanted to be charitable. The last straw for many of them was being commanded to put Ex-Lax on discarded dog food to keep hungry Koreans from returning for more. The excessive waste of it all was impossible to reconcile.

Yet many had done what they could to make the place livable and had sought out beauty and laughter wherever they could. They had defied policy many times, choosing humanity over law, morality over authority. They had grown together and found friendship with their brothers and a filial love for their beloved dogs. Although they wouldn't miss the place, they would miss each other and the men they had become there.

In the last days, their patience wearing thin, many of the men stopped trying to hide their distaste for the authority that held them there. A few of the guys had conspired to show their displeasure by pulling a trick on any officer they encountered. Every time they encountered an officer observing the mission from the security of his Jeep, they would release a dog on him. The handlers would allow the dog to jump on the hood, growling, snarling, and salivating, feigning inability to call the dog off. Only when the handlers thought they had reached the precipice of the officer's patience would they give the dog the word and retract him. The K-9 was always given excessive praise when returning, and the officers couldn't say anything about it. It was policy, after all, always to encourage aggression.

Chan also loved a good game of cat-and-mouse, and he developed his own little subversive game. He detested the way the officers thought they could have access to the dogs whenever they desired, because they were in charge of a dog handling unit. Lieutenant Word, in particular, had a reputation for staying in Seoul and only coming to the units on payday. Many times the men warned the junior officers not to go into the kennels without the escort of a handler, and too often their warnings went unheeded. By the end of his deployment to Korea, Chan had had enough.

One day a young lieutenant, a former airborne paratrooper with zero dog handling experience, walked into the kennel area without regard. Prinz was running loose at the time. Chan knew he wasn't a real danger, but he also knew that Prinz lived to please him. He could ask Prinz to attack, and even if the attack was half-hearted, the officer wouldn't know the difference.

Chan made eye contact with Prinz, who had noticed the stranger in their midst. With a twinkle in his eye, Chan gave the motion and quietly told Prinz, "Get him." Prinz bounded toward the now wide-eyed lieutenant, his barking a terrifying sound to the untrained ear. The officer turned to run, and Prinz leapt for the fleshiest part he could grab, the buttocks. When Prinz returned with a sizable chunk of fabric between his teeth, Chan struggled to choke back the laughter.

"That's a powerful dog you've got there," the lieutenant muttered, almost in tears.

Chan replied, "You have no idea how true that is." After the officer left, Chan praised his dog and even rewarded him with an extra piece of meat. Prinz, feeling loved, lay down with a sigh of satisfaction and was happy.

THE DIFFICULT GOOD-BYE

A few months out from their departure date, the men had started dismantling what they could. When they asked about preparing the kennels for departure, though, they were told to stand down for the moment. A couple weeks before their scheduled return, they started packing their individual belongings, buying souvenirs for loved ones back home, and doing necessary paperwork for leaving the country.

When they inquired about final vet checks for the dogs, though, they were told those would be handled later.

The men had been talking among themselves about all the events of the past months, the success of the patrols in thwarting thievery, the effective riot control, and the kudos received on dog demonstrations. Many became suspicious, especially Paulus and Simpson, who had witnessed the private conversations between U.S. Army officials and ROK authorities firsthand.

The Army had led them to believe, from the beginning, that the dogs would return to Camp Carson after their time was served in Korea. There were no handlers or dogs in training back home—surely that meant the same thing?[1]

The day finally came. The handlers received official orders back to Camp Carson, and they were given three hours to report to the ship for departure. Now it was no longer speculation. The dogs were being left behind. The only decision left for the men of the 8125th was whether or not they would spend those final moments saying good-bye to their dogs. It was a wrenching choice for each of them.

Stewart chose not to go to Duchess or Spooks. He believed his emotion would only affect the entire kennel in a negative way. His choice didn't change the gratitude he had in his heart for the dogs.

Falge elected not to go see Stagmar. He felt it was already hard enough, leaving under those circumstances, to reconcile his feelings. He privately thanked his dog and vowed to remember her sacrifices to the country for the rest of his life.

Fickes sat on his cot stroking the velvety ears of his battle buddy, Katie. Ben, her puppy, was curled in a tight ball, snoozing nearby. He cried, but not so much for Katie and Ben. He had known all along that there was no way they would be returning with him to the states. But he wept for Duke. Duke had given him everything, and now Duke was being betrayed by the country he had served. Fickes thought briefly that if he went to Duke, the dog might think he chose to betray him. He erased that from his mind as soon as it appeared, knowing that Duke had always been able to read his thoughts. He decided to go to him and tell him that he never wanted to leave him. He had no choice.

Simpson went to say good-bye to Grey. He hadn't been surprised by the news, but it still hit him very hard. This day, which he had figured would be the happiest day of his life, had suddenly turned into the saddest. He needed the comfort that only Grey could provide, and he figured that Grey needed him just as much. Simpson sobbed bitter tears into Grey's fur until he could pull himself away.

Hatch went immediately to Willy. He hugged him and kissed him. "I love you so much," he told the dog. "Words can't even begin to say how much." He walked away from Willy and went straight to the bar. Hatch spent his last $50 on booze and got drunk to kill the pain.

Jellison went to the kennel to see Tex, but couldn't bring himself to touch or talk to him. He stood there for a very long time taking in the sight, sound, and smells of the kennel area. He had been forever changed by his dog and couldn't grasp the idea of never seeing him again. He committed on the spot to carrying Tex's portrait, painted by the Korean artisan, everywhere he went. Tex would hang on the walls of any place he called home from that day forward.

Melochik refused to believe that the Army would completely abandon the dogs who had saved countless lives. He worried about who was going to take over Warrior's handling in his absence. He went to tell his friend good-bye but tried not to let him know how he was struggling inside. Instead he chose to walk away from Warrior with a hopeful heart.

Fowler had already endured the pain of separation from his dog, Smokey, many years before as a scout. He could sympathize with what the men were going through, but he could not empathize. He knew Smokey was well loved and cared for after his departure. He had known going to Korea that the dogs wouldn't be coming home. He believed that other handlers would come in to take their spots. Now, who those handler would be, and what qualifications they might have, was ambiguous. He refused to believe the dogs would be abandoned to the local population. That thought was too painful to consider. Not having a dedicated dog of his own, Fowler chose to spend those last moments walking the kennels and giving each dog a word of gratitude for its incredible service. He thought of Smokey, his self-described "pride and joy," and knew that his fellow handlers must be heartbroken.

Broadway went to Rex. He wanted, above all else, to thank him for the protection he had given him on the night of the attack. In spite of Rex's unpredictable ferocity, Broadway took him into his hands, looked him in the eye, and told him, "I don't care what you think, you grumpy old bastard. I'm gonna hug you like you're a beautiful lady." Then he squeezed his dog, caressing his fur, and trying to burn that moment into his memory. Rex took the hug and even seemed, Broadway thought, to return it.

In the end Chan opted not to go to King or Prinz. "It won't change anything," he repeated to himself over and over. Some of the men who had gone to say good-bye to their dogs reported back about Prinz. While all the other dogs were energetic and anxious, Prinz remained calm and collected. He would look up as a new man filed in, but he never offered to get up. The unit's last memories of Prinz would be of him curled up on top of his dog house, back to the breeze, sleeping peacefully. It was as if Prinz was awaiting his next adventure without fear.

Stahlke looked at the document in his hands with wild bewilderment. His eyes scanned page after page, again and again, hoping he had overlooked something. Perhaps headquarters had made a mistake? How could they be returning without the dogs they had been issued at Camp Carson? Surely this was a misunderstanding. The papers fell to the floor as he began wringing his hands. He could feel his heart thudding against his chest. The orders proved what the knot in his stomach had long implied—the dogs were being left behind.

A silence fell over the barracks as one man after another absorbed the words. Stahlke looked at Bakken, then Rath, searching their faces for some recognition of the truth.

"Orion! Are you going to see Bullet?" he pleaded.

Bakken continued to shove clothes into his duffle, face expressionless. Still looking at his pile of belongings, he finally formed a reply. "Damn it, Larry, I don't have time! We have three hours to report. I can't get all this stuff together and still get to the kennels!"

Stahlke swung over to the cot where Rath sat packing.

"You too?" He was enraged.

"You know nothing has ever meant more to me in my life than that dog, but nothing's gonna change the fact that I have to leave him." Rath looked tearful.

"Screw you guys! Those damn dogs gave us everything and you're gonna sit here, leaving them to wonder what the hell happened?! Screw you!" Stahlke raced out the door, filled with rage, slamming it so hard that it sounded like an explosion. His head ached.

The dogs, keenly aware of every human emotion and alert to every expression and gesture that their handlers made, knew that this day was different. There was an anxious buzz hovering over the dog yard, very different from the normal frenetic energy they usually displayed. Their yips had turned to sharp cries of separation. Their barks had become mournful howls.

Stahlke slowed down, realizing his run could spook one of the more aggressive dogs and cause him to turn and attack. He went to Junker like he had done a million times before. He knew that Junker would be looking for him as he always did: perched on top of his house, tail wagging, spinning in excited circles. Stahlke wondered how he would explain all of this to his greatest friend and partner.

Junker was at once toddler child and killer beast. He could fall into a puddle of pure love and admiration at the sight of his best friend and handler, then turn and rip out another man's throat at the flick of a wrist. But Junker was so keenly aware of Stahlke's emotions that no words were needed. Today, as Junker saw his best friend, he was quiet. He came to lie at Stahlke's feet, exposing his vulnerable underbelly for a rub. Stahlke grabbed the scruff of Junker's neck and, bringing his face down to meet him, looked deeply into his black eyes.

"You're a good boy, Junker. There will never be a boy as good as you."

He took his time stroking the length of Junker's body, separating his fingers to feel the sensation of his soft black and tan coat one last time.

"I can't stay, boy."

Junker whimpered.

"I love you, boy. There will never be another dog like you." Standing in a single crisp movement, the way a soldier will, Stahlke faced Junker and gave him the "Sit" command. Junker obediently sat. Looking into Junker's eyes, he gave his loyal friend the hardest command he would ever have to speak. "Stay."

Stahlke struggled for air over the lump in his throat. He turned and walked away, gasping and feeling Junker's eyes on him, until he was out of sight.

It would be a year before Stahlke would learn what ultimately happened to Junker that day, the day of their final goodbye. Back home in South Dakota, he would receive a letter from the vet-tech responsible for the transition of the dogs to the Republic of Korea Army. The letter stated simply:

> Junker, once you were out of sight, began jumping as high as the chain would allow. We tried to soothe him but he would not be calmed. He jumped until he collapsed, not from exhaustion but all of a sudden. Without the benefit of an autopsy we cannot say for sure what killed him. It seems however that his heart just gave out, and he stopped breathing.

13

THE GREAT ESCAPE

A few weeks before the actual orders came down to the 8125th, Broadway had clearly seen the writing on the wall. The knowledge that the dogs weren't returning to Camp Carson had felt like a sucker punch to the gut. How could the Army turn its back on any of the dogs, especially Rex, who had done exactly what they had trained him to do? He couldn't prove that the Army had made a secret deal with the ROK Army for transfer of the dogs, but he had seen enough to draw the conclusion in his own mind. As a vet-tech, he had kept up with all the necessary health certificates and vaccinations for the dogs, and he had witnessed a keen interest from ROK officials in that paperwork over the past several weeks. He also noticed that the U.S. Army showed no similar interest, which was odd considering the dogs were supposed to be re-entering the country. Surely the Army should want proof of health?

Broadway had understood, too, through the multiple requests he received, that the ROK Army was only interested in the healthiest and most desirable dogs. He thought of Blind Sam and burned with righteous indignation. He wondered if the dogs not used by the ROK Army would end up as meals for the hungry Koreans waiting just outside the gate. At least the dogs like Rex, who would surely make the transition to the ROK, had a chance. If for no other reason, they wouldn't be carved up because of the money invested in getting them. But Sam was a different story.

Broadway was never one to turn a blind eye to a living creature in need. His Texas upbringing had taught him that all life was valuable, and it was the highest calling to protect the innocent whenever possible. He struggled with the guilt of having taken a life, even by proxy, and placed a penance on himself as a result. Never again would he refuse to help someone in need. And Sam was more than "someone" to him; he was Broadway's friend. He wanted to save all the dogs, but rationality prevailed. Broadway accepted that he could only do what he could do. He thought of Sam's buddy Prinz with sadness, but Prinz with his good nature and good health would certainly survive. Without hesitation, Broadway devised a plan and committed to put it into action the next day.

It would be easy to get Sam away from the kennels without notice. He had, after all, tagged along with Broadway unfettered for many months. If anyone asked about the dog's whereabouts that day, Broadway was going to tell them that he had been very sick and was being treated inside the tent. He had managed to secure a truck and a large canvas tarp for the journey. He knew that he could trust Sam to keep quiet going out of the gate. All he had to do was put Sam in a "stay" in the back and throw the tarp over him. Anyway, if he got caught carrying Sam off the property he would say that he was taking him to the only vet around, in Seoul, and that would coincide with the ruse he concocted about Sam's illness. Broadway then falsified a death certificate with Sam's name and date of death.

It was late in the day when Broadway and Sam finally hit the road. Broadway had waited until business died down on post, and he could usher Sam into the truck with little or no notice. When the moment arrived, he was nervous and a little giddy. He looked at Sam and told him, "I don't give a damn what I've got to do, you're going home today!" Sam wagged his tail.

Maybe it was the excitement that clouded his awareness, but the two were not, as Broadway had thought, unnoticed. Simpson had come to the vet tent in need of something for Grey. He watched Sam jump onto the truck, witnessed the loving exchange between Broadway and his beloved dog, and continued inside to get the supplies he needed for himself. Inside, he noticed it: Broadway had left the fake death certificate out in plain view. Simpson smiled and vowed to keep this wonderful secret all to himself.

The truck rumbled down the road for a while, until Broadway felt certain that they were out of sight. At that point he got out and invited Sam into the cab so the two friends could spend their last hour together, sitting side by side. As they drove, Broadway told Sam how happy his new life was going to be and how much he was going to miss him. Sam rested his head on Broadway's lap.

As they drove up to the orphanage, Sam's excitement began to build. He loved this place, the missionary, the children. His smell memory had activated at least a mile out, and the anticipation was building. Every time they had visited in the past, he had been lavished with love and treats, and it had created a good and lasting memory. Broadway's heart felt like it would explode as he saw Sam become more and more joyful. Before he could throw the truck into park, the kids were bursting through the door, running at the vehicle, laughing, and calling Sam's name.

The missionary met the pair in the driveway, and the two men embraced while Sam ran playful circles around everyone. Broadway had brought enough horse meat and dog food to last Sam for a long time. He had even managed to sneak out enough to give the children a few good meals as well. The missionary assured Broadway that Sam had a safe and lasting home at the orphanage. Sam would live the rest of his days in complete freedom. He would be granted total access, never on a chain again, allowed to roam the grounds or stay in the classroom as he liked. Most importantly, the missionary promised Broadway that Sam would be loved until the end of his days.

Broadway knew that he had done the very best thing for Sam and the orphans. He called the dog to him one last time before leaving. "Old Blind Sam, get over here!" Sam trotted over, tongue lolling out of his mouth from delightful exertion. Broadway made eye contact with Sam for the last time, "You be a good boy, okay, buddy?" Sam licked at Broadway's face, an affirmation that he would always try to be just that.

Broadway returned to post with a smile from ear to ear. He wondered if perhaps he should try to hide his happiness, since he technically just "put down" his old friend. And then there was the matter of stealing government property and falsifying government documents, which could bring harsh and lifelong consequences if he were caught. "I don't give a damn," Broadway decided. "Let them question me all they want. I'm not sorry and I'd do it again."

The next morning he filed the death certificate and went on about his day.

14

CALLING THE PACK

The men boarded the ship bound for home in November 1955, torn between two worlds. For almost two years they had been intimately linked with their dogs, spending nearly all their time together. Over time they had learned every nuance of one another. The dogs had become more than just their right hands. They were connected on a wavelength that was incomprehensible. Although the men still had one another, each man felt alone and incomplete.

Still, they were excited to return to the comforts of home. They missed their families. They had longed to escape the destitution of Korea and be, once again, in a loving place sheltered from the cold and the misery. The men didn't regret the bonds they had formed with each other and with their cherished K-9s, even if it meant heartbreak in the end, but they did look forward to home and what they believed would be a safe haven from the pain.

The voyage home took about twenty days. They had to get through typhoons, sea-sickness, and—of course—chores. (Broadway and Chan got the garbage detail instead of KP this time.) On this voyage, though, unlike their journey to Korea, there were no dogs to tend. This left a serious void, and boredom set in quickly. The only break in the monotony was a brief stop to resupply in Adak Island, Alaska. Before they got there, Fickes asked one of the ship's crew if there were any girls in Adak.

"Oh yes," he replied. "There's one behind every tree."

He was being sarcastic, of course.

When the ship finally arrived in San Francisco harbor in mid-December, the men were ready to enjoy their hard-earned rest. They would travel by bus to Fort Ord for in-processing before receiving leave just in time for Christmas. Many of the men, like Stewart, were released at Fort Ord because their enlistment time was up, but others still had time left in service. Of the ones still left with time to serve, a small group, which included Fickes and Hatch (who eventually transferred into the Air Force), stayed in the Army and made a career out of it.

The men had become brothers. They knew that now they would go their separate ways, and though it was an exciting time for all of them, they realized this meant they would be dividing the 8125th family once again. They vowed to keep in touch. The men agreed they owed it to the dogs to stay intact as best they could.

Stewart arrived home on Christmas Eve. The time together with his family was good, but he couldn't deny that he missed his friends. His plan after getting out of the Army was to go to college and maybe even play football. He didn't know when or how he would see them all again, but he looked forward to that day.

Fickes stayed at Camp Carson for a while after returning from Korea. The Army dog training program there had been amalgamated with the Twenty-Fifth Infantry Scout Dog Platoon, and Fickes carried on with his dog training career.[1] There were no sentries to train, but Fickes had proven himself in obedience handling so he was chosen to be a part of the unit's demonstration team instead. In that job, he went around with a Doberman Pinscher and a Cocker Spaniel, showing America that war dogs have lots of different capabilities besides guarding and attack. In fact, it was these dogs that proved once again to American military brass that the scouting abilities of dogs were an invaluable asset to our national defense. They would be the reason that all branches of the service would eventually adopt large-scale scout dog programs in the future. And it was the Labrador retrievers and German Shepherds who were later adopted into this training program, who saved countless lives in Vietnam with their tracking, sniffing, and bomb detecting capabilities.

A few months after getting back to Camp Carson, Fickes received a letter from a vet-tech named Jewel Lingus, who had remained behind after the 8125th left Korea. Reporting on Duke, Lingus wrote that the dog had a good handler (likely a member of the Military Police, not a trained handler, who took on the dog unofficially) and was doing well. This brought Fickes some peace of mind. As he read on though, he discovered the true purpose of the letter. Lingus wrote, "I hate to have to tell you this, but I know you would want to know. Katie and Ben were very lonely without you and couldn't be controlled. Someone shot and killed them. It was probably better for them in the end anyway."

Fickes's heart broke all over again. He knew Katie could be controlled. She had, after all, slept in his tent, under his bunk. Ben had slept in his own dog house in the kennel compound, shaded from the summer sun and insulated against the cold winter months. Neither of the dogs was ever any meaner than the rest of the sentries. Katie and Ben had been valuable assets to the 8125th, and this disregard for their service was more than Fickes could stand. From that bitter moment on, his heart was no longer in handling dogs. In December 1956, he was released from active duty in the United States Army. He went on to use his GI Bill for school and to buy a little house in Colorado. He married, divorced, and then married the love his life, Pat, who had two kids of her own. He worked in the Post Office and eventually retired from there. But the hole he had in his heart from leaving his dogs in Korea—and especially from knowing what happened to Katie and Ben—left him lonely for someone who could understand the depth of that grief.

Benevenga had left Katie and Ben in Fickes's care when he left Korea. His military working dog had been handed over to one of the other very competent handlers in the 8125th. After being treated for his burns in Japan, he went back to the United States and was honorably discharged from the Army. After leaving the Army, he went back to school as he had always planned. But Benevenga never worried about his dogs because he knew they were in good hands. He even thought he might be able to return to Camp Carson in a year or two and visit Grey. He never did return, however, because he moved on with life, and as he would learn many years later, Grey and the other dogs never returned.

Ben went on to earn a Ph.D. in nutritional science. He did post-doctoral work at MIT and later become a professor of animal sciences at the University of Wisconsin, Madison. He and his wife settled there, and he conducted ground-breaking research on the metabolism of baby pigs, which would later benefit human preemies. But

Benevenga often wondered about the place he had left in such a hurry and the dear friends, canine and human, who had helped form his character and changed his life forever. It was easy to lose touch with his brothers as life took them in different directions, but he missed them. In an attempt to reconnect, he went back to Korea to see if he could feel the ghosts of the men and dogs he had shared that space with so long ago.

Simpson came home and got out of the Army at the end of his enlistment. He used his GI Bill to attend graduate school for chemical engineering. While in school he met a beautiful girl named Shirley, who talked about horses and her dream to have a farm of her own. She also talked incessantly about her sorority's mascot, a giant, ill-mannered oaf of a St. Bernard. None of the girls had been able to do anything with the dog. He slobbered and peed wherever he pleased, mowed people over when excited, and in general wouldn't do a thing he was told. She knew that Simpson had been a dog handler in Korea and asked him if he thought anything could be done about the beast. Wanting to get a little extra time with her, Simpson guaranteed that if he spent enough time with the dog, he could whip him into shape.

The dog was incorrigible, and despite all his skills Simpson was only ever able to make the dog manageable. But his lack of complete success with the mascot didn't cause the girl to lose interest in him. In fact, Simpson and the girl fell in love, and a few years later they got married, bought a farm, and had a few kids, horses, and dogs to make the place home.

Simpson always retained his love for dogs, but he never stopped comparing them to Grey. No dog ever matched the level of love and respect he had for his old partner. Over the years he thought about Grey and the demonstration he performed for the general. He wondered if Grey ever made it the general's complex or if he wasted away in the kennels, looking for Simpson's return.

Chan got out of the Army at the end of his enlistment and moved back to California near his family. He met a woman named Leonore and they had two kids. The romance which once had seemed so promising between Chan and Mary Jay had proven to be nothing more than a flirtation. This was fully realized when Chan met Leonore, whom he would call the love of his life. He worked a job until retirement and then, in spite of having cancer, lived his life to the fullest. He thought about the guys often and wondered where life had taken them. Because of the power he had witnessed in the sentry dogs, he never connected with a dog again.

Mary Jay Osler had lost contact with Chan while he was still in Korea. He had many flirtations then, and the absence of her letters went largely unnoticed by him. He remembered her, though, throughout his life, because she had been his connection to Prinz. For her, school and extra-curricular activities, even other boys (as her father had feared) drew her away from her interest in the handler and Prinz. She went on, after high school, to pursue a career in acting, and she even ended up on Broadway and worked with stars like Peter Ustinov, Christopher Plummer, and Joanne Woodward. Mary Jay regarded Pete with nostalgic fondness throughout the years, telling people she knew, "I think I might have been in love with him."

Hatch made a career out of the military, but not in the Army. After returning from Korea, he was supposed to work with the scout dogs at Carson, but a surprise change of orders diverted him to the First Infantry Division at Fort Riley, Kansas, instead. He had heard many times that the Air Force treated their personnel better than the Army. After the bad taste left in his mouth by Korea, he was inclined to believe that to be true. So after getting an honorable discharge from the Army, he joined the Utah Air National Guard in 1958. In the Guard he worked on NORAD radar sites and developed a skill set which would be in high demand in the Vietnam War. In 1968 he was called to active duty and sent to Thailand as a radar tech in support of the country's mission in Vietnam. He retired from the Air Force as a master sergeant after almost thirty years of combined military service.

In 1975 Hatch met his wife, an American school teacher on Ramstein Air Force Base, Germany. He had three children from a previous marriage, but Hatch and Dalene never had kids. Instead, they had several small breed dogs throughout their life together, who were just as much their babies as any human could have been. Hatch loved his little dogs. He could never consider having another German Shepherd—the breed always reminded him of Willy, and it was difficult for him to think about "replacing" him.

Melochick stayed in the Army and made a career of it. After returning home, he transferred from the Doggies to Logistics, went to Vietnam in the 1970s, and retired after more than twenty years. In spite of his poor family life as a child, Melochick managed to raise a close-knit family of his own. The Army had given him the rearing that he had not had growing up, providing him stability, financial peace, and an education to support his family. For that, he gave the service all the credit. He felt molded, although sometimes by fire, as a soldier. The brothers he had in the 8125th were a natural extension of that family, and he thought of them often throughout the years. Because of his time in Korea with Warrior, he kept dogs in his family circle too.

Broadway was discharged from the Army at Fort Ord right after returning from Korea. He flew home to Texas right away and was there to spend Christmas with his family. Less than a month after getting home, he found a great job at a local bank and worked his way up in the company as an appraiser, then a loan officer, then a building inspector, until he started handling investments. In 1957 he married his sweetheart, Pat, and they had three children, one of which was stillborn. Broadway lost Pat to a sudden and unexpected brain hemorrhage in 1976. Two years after Pat's death, he married a woman he had counted as a friend for twenty years, Gerry. After they married he told everyone he had been twice blessed with two wonderful women.

Broadway thought of the men he had served with in the 8125th often. He wondered if he would ever see them again, especially Chan, and hoped they were all well. He managed over time to keep the dead Korean out of his thoughts. He chose instead to celebrate life. Remembering Sam, and how he had left him happy and cared for in Korea, was always a source of comfort to him. He never told anyone his secret, preferring to keep that sweet memory all to himself.

Fowler stayed in the military for a few more years, then got out and went to college in Backus, Minnesota, in 1966. After college he took a mining job, where he worked for twenty years. When he retired from mining, he continued to work maintenance for the town of Embarrass, Minnesota, for another twenty-two years. In the meantime he found a passion for weather observation and began reporting for nationally syndicated programs such as Jimmy Kimmel, Brian Matthew, and Garrison Keillor. Community service also held a valuable place in his life. He served on the school board, the town fair board, and the credit union board. Fowler continued to serve his fellow veterans by honoring them in the color guard at funerals.

One month after getting out of the Army, Fowler bought a dog, a Golden Retriever. He couldn't imagine life without one by his side. Dogs had saved his life in Korea, and they had been the most loyal companions he had ever known. This retriever, the best hunting dog he ever had, was the first in a long line of dogs to come. Fowler lost contact with the other handlers after coming home from Korea, but through his fellowship with other dogs throughout his life, he felt like he would always have a connection to Smokey.

Paulus left Korea after eighteen months, remaining there a few months longer than the rest, and came home in the summer of 1956. At Siheung, South Korea, where Paulus and Fritz ended up, the kennels were a half mile from the barracks. With the time constraint, there was no way he could get to his dog to say good-bye and be at the ship on time. His heart ached as he thought of Fritz languishing in the kennels, and a wave of immense guilt washed over him. He was filled with rage at the Army for forcing this horrific situation on him.

Paulus knew, having worked on the demo team, that the dogs would end up in the hands of the Koreans. In the years following his time in Korea, he dealt with sadness and rage over what happened to the dogs. He moved on with life as best he could, going to college, marrying Corrine, and having three beautiful children. Over the years he worked in a wide variety of career fields, even becoming a Methodist minister later in life.

Still, Fritz haunted him. The former dog handler couldn't consider getting another dog for a long time because it felt like a betrayal. As he got older, however, he started to realize that the very presence of a dog, a German Shepherd specifically, might be what he needed to heal and reconcile with what had happened. He started looking into adopting a former military working dog through the Air Force's Military Working Dog (MWD) adoption program. As a former handler he should have had preference, but other factors trumped that, especially his advanced age, and he was denied adoption privileges.[2] He was crushed all over again.

Paulus prayed about what he should do, asking God to give him a sign or send him a message. Not long after this, the message barreled into his life in the form of a German Shepherd. She literally bounded into his living room and sat at his feet. She was beautiful, and Paulus figured she must belong to someone. Sure enough, his local vet had her in the system. She was a neighbor's dog who had gotten loose. Paulus had hoped to keep her, but he wasn't as downtrodden as he thought he might be, having to give her back. Instead, the dog made him hopeful. He started looking into German Shepherd rescues, and within months he welcomed a dog into his home. She was a perfect match for their family with her gentle spirit. She also needed the guidance and nurturing Paulus was expert at giving to dogs. He knew that giving this wonderful dog a good home was a way of honoring Fritz.

Batson went to Colorado. Wooden went home to California. So did Falge. Slaughter took off in a direction no one knew. The last anyone heard, he had gone to Texas. Garfield was rumored to have married and gone to live in a remote cabin in Alaska. Mardunkle, from what the other handlers gleaned over the years, went home and drank himself to death. Another handler, Garner, made a high-profile career out of his dog-handling skills. He went to Hollywood after Korea and trained dogs for the show *Green Acres*. Later in life he would train several dogs to fill the role of Beethoven in the series of movies by the same name.

Gerry Ballanger, Prinz's first owner, remained in Bangor, Maine. He worked as a high school guidance counselor for many years, choosing a meager salary in order to work with kids. His salary never allowed for training and showing dogs as he had dreamed. Prinz was the first of his dogs to be sold to the military; two more followed after him. Most significant of the other dogs was Pharaoh, Prinz's son.

Pharaoh was inducted into the United States Air Force about a year after his sire went into the Army. He also worked as a sentry dog, and his handler, Airman Samuel Yoder, once told Gerry, "Pharaoh was the best sentry dog that ever lived." Pharaoh remained stateside, in North Carolina, throughout his career, transferring to at least one more handler after Yoder.

Yoder had bonded on a deep level with Pharaoh and hoped to bring him home for retirement when he was no longer able to work. However, according to new military policy, Military Working Dogs were considered surplus equipment, which would stay in America's defense arsenal until death.[3]

BAKKEN, PETERSON, RATH, AND STAHLKE

Bakken returned to his regular life in Milan, Minnesota, after Korea. He married his sweetheart and had kids. The couple also had dogs. Weimaraners, with their quiet and aloof disposition, became the family's favorite breed. His time with the Military Working Dogs had given Bakken a healthy respect for dogs and what they were capable of. He kept his distance from all dogs he didn't know because he had seen firsthand the destructive power a dog can unleash on an unfamiliar man. He never wanted to risk being that victim.

Bakken and Rath had been best friends throughout their time in Korea. Many people, seeing them together, thought they were brothers. After Korea they went their separate ways, but they promised to stay in contact, which they did. Almost every day Bakken thought about his brothers, especially Rath, and wondered what had become of them. Once on a trip to Black Hills, South Dakota, Bakken saw a highway sign pointing travelers to Laurel, Nebraska. It was close. Bakken told his wife, Kitty, that Rath was from that town. He wondered, "What are the chances he's still there?" Kitty gave him the look of approval he had grown to understand. He told her, "I've got to try."

The couple drove into the parking lot of what looked like a popular Laurel restaurant. Bakken figured it was such a small town, the kind where everybody knows everybody else's business, that the chances were excellent someone would know Eddie Rath. It was no surprise to find many people who did know Rath and his family. The surprise was that Rath and his wife, Judy, had moved to the big city of Omaha. Bakken went back home committed to continuing his search.

It was in this search for Rath that Bakken developed an idea. The men had been such a huge part of each other's lives, and he knew that he couldn't be the only one who missed that fraternity. He thought of the dogs and how difficult it had been to leave them. It was a thought that had crossed his mind many times throughout the years. He knew that only his fellow handlers could understand the shared suffering of Korea, and leaving the dogs behind. Bakken came to a conclusion: they needed a reunion to heal and be whole again. He would start his search for his brothers with the information he had about Rath living in Omaha.

It took two years to find him. When Bakken finally reached Rath by telephone, the two were elated. They made plans for Rath to come up to Bakken's house and plan a reunion. When the two men finally got together, they reminisced for five straight hours. They pulled out boxes of photos and told old stories. They formed a solid plan to pull the men together again. Bakken knew where Stahlke was in North Dakota, and both men were sure they knew where to find Peterson; he had never gone far from the little hometown he and Bakken shared.

Eddie and Judy Rath shared a long and sweet marriage. They only had one minor argument, in fact, during their many years together.

Rath could be very conservative, and honest to a fault, which some people could find offensive. But he loved his family and friends in such a way that he would move heaven and earth to help them. Judy often laughed at her Eddie, who could remember every detail of the life he shared with the men and dogs of the 8125th but had a hard time remembering the names of people he had been acquainted with for decades. He loved those men and dogs, and both had earned his life-long devotion.

When Rath called Stahlke and told him about the plans for a reunion, the reserved former handler, who never did much outside the family home, blurted out in pure joy, "I'll be there!" His wife, Mary-Ann, was shocked to hear his reaction, but she knew that he had a soft spot for the men and the dogs. She felt it would be good for him and supported his going every step of the way. She had heard the story about Junker jumping to get to his handler until he died of a broken heart many times. She knew that her husband needed to fill the hole that tragic ending had left in his life. It had haunted him, but he had shared it with no one else. She could see it come out from time to time, like when he asked the couple's son-in-law to put down his beloved mini Collie; he couldn't stand the horrific memories he knew that act would trigger. MaryAnn hoped that he could release those demons in the safety of the brotherhood.

Rath and Bakken next went in search of Peterson. They started by walking into a small dive bar, somewhere between Milan and Arcadia, Wisconsin, joking that there probably was not a bar in that county Peterson had not graced with his presence.

Rath announced, "I'm looking for a Curt Peterson. Anybody know him?"

A woman sitting at the bar turned around with a smile. "Curt Peterson is my dad." She called him right then. Peterson then led them to another member of the 8125th who had been his best friend in Korea, Leonard Pierzyna.

Pierzyna lived in the small town of Arcadia, Wisconsin, not too far from Milan. Rath and Bakken set out right away for Arcadia. Driving down a residential street, not knowing exactly where to start, they saw a mail carrier standing by a residential mailbox. The men discussed it and agreed that if anyone would know a name like Pierzyna, it would be a postal employee. They approached the woman, startling her a little and causing her to look at them suspiciously.

Bakken spoke to her first, with his trademark twinkle. "Hey we're looking for a guy that we figure is the town drunk."

The woman smiled.

"Do you know a Leonard Pierzyna?" Rath asked.

Catching both men completely off-guard, the woman hugged them. "That's my husband. And who the hell are you?"

The men's explanation for why they were there brought tears to the woman's eyes. She told them that her husband was in a nursing home and not doing well. She would tell him right away all about how the men were coming together again, but she didn't know if he would understand. Dementia had ravaged his mind at that point. But before he fell ill, he had talked all the time about Korea, and the men and the dogs. Later the men would find out that Pierzyna had heard and understood. He was delighted that the men would be together again. He even hoped a miracle might happen so he could be there, too. Sadly, that did not happen. He died not long after, but he had peace knowing that his brotherhood was still intact.

From these initial first contacts, word of the reunion spread. Most of the handlers had kept in touch with at least one of their closest friends throughout the years and would pass the word along. Some men, however, would never be found. They had vanished into their own lives, maybe removed from what happened in Korea, but most likely not unaffected. Garfield felt no connection to the men and dogs and refused to attend.

Slaughter, the only black man in the unit, had always felt segregated. Poole had been close to him in Korea but now was unable to reach out to him. Falge did reach Slaughter and extended an invitation to the reunion, but Slaughter declined. He felt he didn't belong.

Chan didn't find out about this inaugural reunion until a couple years later. It was no fault of his own. He had not been hiding and was missing them as much as they missed him. The search for him had gone down many false paths because his brothers were searching for someone under the wrong name—it was an identity they had created for him during their time together, and not the actual person. In fact, they had called him "Chin" for so long that Chan had started referring to himself that way, every time he talked about Korea.

15

HOME

The first reunion of the 8125th Korea 1954–1955, held in Omaha, Nebraska, in 2004, included nearly half of the original dog handlers. The wives came along, and over the years sometimes adult children also came, hoping to learn more about this mysterious and influential part of their loved ones' lives.

Most of the men agreed that their time in Korea had affected their entire lives. It made them different. Whatever age they might have been when they came to the 8125th, all said that they "grew up" in Korea. It had been a transforming experience. The stories that unfolded on that first night in 2004 gave many of the family members the answers they had long sought. It was the first time many of the men felt safe to talk about the realities of war. It was the first time many were able to discuss the atrocious poverty they witnessed in Korea, and the hardship of being so bonded with a dog and then having that most trusted partner and friend ripped from them in an instant.

The men recalled the funny stories, too. Fickes had been a child in Korea, and he was the one who grew up the most. Broadway and Chan had always kept everybody in stitches. Everyone was surprised that Garfield made it out alive. Hatch told everyone about letting the dog loose on the two lovers in the Jeep. Although the laughter rolled on, as one man after another recounted some hilarious tale, they all knew that these were more than humorous anecdotes. These were the stories of their survival.

Having focused the entire evening on the experiences that the men shared among themselves, Paulus became visibly irritated. He needed to interject, to mention the elephant in the room and remind everyone that they wouldn't be there if it were not for the dogs. "You're eighteen years old and you get your dog and your life is changed forever. Those dogs offered to lay down their lives for us every day."

On the last night of their four-day reunion, at the closing ceremony, Stewart shared something he had written to honor the men and dogs of the 8125th. He had created a roll call, "A Tribute to the Silent Sentries." These were the names of the men and dogs who had already passed on. Like Paulus, he recognized that they owed their lives, and the lives of the resulting generations, to the dogs.

During the same closing ceremony, Hatch presented the men with a ritual. It was to be kept as an honored tradition until the very last reunion. A fine bottle of cognac was opened and each man presented a shot. They would, as a group, pray and give thanks for those who had gone before. They would read the roll call of the silent sentries, and in the end they would swallow the shot in memory of the family members, canine and human, who had gone before them. They agreed that the last man standing, at the last reunion, would drink the last bottle of cognac dry. Finally, someone found and read an anonymous poem befitting the occasion and honoring the dogs called "Guardians of the Night."

AFTERWORD

No one can say for certain what happened to the dogs of the 8125th. It was rumored that the very best would go to the Republic of Korea Army, but no one ever actually saw the transition. The men hoped that at least the dogs with warrior prowess, like Simpson's Grey, got picked up. They knew all too well that to the Koreans, even the best examples of military working dogs would never be trusted friends and companions, but only military weapons to be feared. "Tame" dogs like Stewart's Duchess and Chan's Prinz probably never had a chance.

In 2015, however, Harlan received the most promising news any of the men had yet heard regarding the fate of the dogs in Korea. Chuck Powell reached what had been the 8125th at Yong Dong Po shortly after the men had been forced to leave their beloved K-9 partners behind. He was an MP whose duty was to guard the perimeter of the remaining American property on that installation. When he arrived, he found a few beautiful and attentive German Shepherds hanging around the area. He was told they had once been sentry dogs for the 8125th. Powell, a dog lover who wasn't excited about the thought of long night patrols alone, decided to take one of the friendliest of the dogs along with him. He later told Harlan that the dog became a great friend, and he hated that he had to leave him behind when his rotation in Korea was finished.

By 1956, one small pocket of military dog training continued in Showa (Tachikawa), Japan, supplying dogs to the Asian theater.[1] Their role remained primarily that of sentry dogs until the beginning of American involvement in Vietnam. In 1964, the standard dog training had moved to Lackland Air Force Base, Texas, and sentries, scouts, and patrol/detection dogs were all utilized in the conflict. The Army still viewed the dogs as nothing more than military equipment, so there was no exact count kept of the dogs sent into the war zone until 1968. The official count of dogs (those tattooed and fully accounted for) who served in Vietnam is 3,747. It is believed that the actual number is closer to 5,000 across all branches of the armed forces. Close to 10,000 dog handlers deployed with the dogs, making the ten years of American involvement in Vietnam the greatest concentrated effort of military working dogs in the nation's history. Of the nearly 5,000 dogs in Vietnam, only 204 left; none ever returned to civilian life. Most were either euthanized or turned over to the South Vietnamese Army (ARVN). Sadly, the Vietnamese saw the dogs just as the Koreans had: they feared them and did not trust them.[2]

As American involvement in foreign wars continued throughout the years, dogs remained present, guarding and protecting American interests at home and abroad. During Operation Desert Storm and

Desert Shield, 118 Military Working Dog teams were deployed.[3] By this time the U.S. military had learned some lessons about the care and treatment of dogs, and the policy was that the dogs would return with their handlers to the bases and posts from which they came at the end of their service. This wasn't hard to accomplish, since the ground war was short-lived.

Still, the question remained: what was the life of a military working dog worth to the Department of Defense? Were the dogs still considered military equipment? The handlers who bonded with them on unimaginably deep levels knew that these dogs were fellow soldiers, friends, and invaluable tools who deserved a good quality of life. Military brass and bureaucracy had not yet come full circle in recognizing the needs and rights of military working dogs.

By September 11, 2001, the nation had become more aware of the invaluable service of military working dogs. Dogs sifted tirelessly through the rubble at Ground Zero, and soon after more dogs went to war, protecting our sons and daughters in Afghanistan and Iraq. Science had also, by this time, illustrated some truths about dogs which our nation's dog handlers already knew. By now science had given us a much better idea of just how vast a dog's emotional and intellectual IQ truly is. Now we understand that separation anxiety is equally as devastating for a dog as it is for a human child at age two.[4] Researchers also began to understand that post-traumatic stress is a very real problem for dogs who serve in war, or in a tragedy such as 9/11. Moreover, researchers began to publish findings that dogs have an unrivaled therapeutic success rate for humans who suffer from PTSD. Despite the publication of these findings and growing public awareness, dogs were still being left in war zones, separated from their handlers or brought home and not allowed to retire.

In 1983, former scout dog handler Master Sergeant (Ret.) John C. Burnam left the Army, but he could never leave the memories of his time in Vietnam with his dogs, Clipper and Timber. At the end of his service in Vietnam, he had been ordered simply to walk away from Clipper. His heartbreaking story was not unique. Thousands of dog handlers had faced this heartbreaking situation on leaving their tour of duty. In his retirement, Burnam decided to take action and bring honor to the dogs. For thirty years he sought out legislators who were sympathetic to the plight of military working dogs and handlers. He wanted to build a national monument to honor the service of canines and handlers, across all branches of service, breeds, and wars in which they had served.

The dedication of the National Monument of U.S. Military Working Dog Teams took place on October 28, 2013, at Lackland Air Force Base. Thousands attended the opening, and it was an incredible moment for those who had loved and lost, as well as those who continued to work with dogs. Three years later, almost to the day, the remaining men of the 8125th met at Lackland for their sixty-first annual reunion. The sight of the monument brought tears to their eyes. At last their dogs had received the recognition they deserved for their service to our nation.

In Burnam's pursuit of a national monument, many issues facing military working dogs and handlers came to light. These issues were brought to Capitol Hill for resolution. Dogs and handlers were still being senselessly separated. Many dogs, in spite of their inability to perform their assigned jobs (perhaps because they had become "tame" or had suffered PTSD) were kept on until they died or had to be euthanized. For many years, dogs with military experience were sold to police stations throughout the United States so they could continue working. This was not always a bad thing, as the dogs brought unmatched expertise to the job, but often the dogs were physically spent after years of demanding work. Americans began to call for legislation to remedy these problems.

As a result, today military working dogs are better protected and cared for. Legislation ensures they will never be left behind or abandoned again. The Air Force's 341st Training Squadron, Thirty-Seventh Training Wing, is now the permanent home of all MWD training, breeding, and adoptions of former (and wash-out) K-9s. The standard of training is set at Lackland, and the dogs are closely monitored for service in all branches of service and federal law enforcement agencies. A stringent breeding program is in place there, and the qualities most valued in MWDs are fostered and nurtured. If a dog doesn't make it through training, there are adoption procedures, monitored and maintained by the 341st, to ensure the dogs find healthy forever homes. The dogs returning from service are now

An eternal brotherhood.

The dogs: the Silent Sentries of the 8125th Sentry Dog Detachment Korea. They were loved beyond measure.

offered up for adoption so they can retire and live the rest of their lives in comfort. Former handlers have priority for adoption.

———

The men of the 8125th and their family members continue their annual reunions, though sadly, with each passing year the list of attendees dwindles. Chan lost his wife, Leonore, in 2016. Simpson also recently passed away. Many of the men are dealing bravely with serious health issues. All continue to live their lives with dignity and courage. No one knows when the last reunion will be, but the bottle of cognac will be there, and the roll call of the Silent Sentries will be read. Now, even when that last reunion is over, the memories of the men and dogs of the 8125th will live on.

NOTES

All photos are courtesy of the personal collections of the men of the 8125th Sentry Dog Detachment Korea.

ONE: WAR DOGS

1. Michael G. Lemish, *War Dogs: A History of Loyalty and Heroism* (Washington D.C.: Brassey's Press, 1996), 1. Michael Lemish's *War Dogs* gives a general history of Military Working Dogs throughout history focusing mainly on the role of war dogs during WWII and Vietnam.
2. Susan Orlean, *Rin Tin Tin: The Life and the Legend* (New York: Simon and Schuster, 2011), 149.
3. The so-called most aggressive breeds, and the breeds ultimately used most frequently in WWII, were the Doberman Pinscher (used mainly in the

Pacific for scouting) and the German Shepherd (used mostly in the U.S., and by the Coast Guard, for sentry duty).

4. Lemish, 41.

5. Lemish, 145.

6. Lemish, 143. The official statement from Dogs for Defense at the end of the war read, "We feel that the place for a K9 veteran is in a home and not in some kennel or an Army post." Lemish explains that the War Department finally came out with official policy in 1945 regarding the disposal of "surplus dogs." Their disposal should be handled in the following order: 1. They could be issued to Seeing Eye Inc as perspective seeing eye dogs. 2. They could be issued to a military organization as a mascot. 3. Dogs could be made available to servicemen who had handled them in service. 4. They could be sold by the Procurement Division of the Treasury Department. Lemish goes on to say, "Although DFD offered its services to place all surplus dogs not returned to their original owners, by law, as government property, they needed to be sold." This idea of dogs being equipment, instead of living beings, would plague the U.S. military until modern times.

7. Hut Vass was a small boy when this Doberman was alive. The story comes from his personal oral history and he was unable to remember the dog's name. He could, however, vividly remember the dog sitting quietly at church, waiting for his Grandmother to arrive.

8. The Danville Register Bee Fritz Takes Up Residence After Army Service.

9. Private breeders were, by the beginning of the Korean War, offered $100 for a single dog if that dog fit their guidelines for temperament and conformation.

10. Risch and Keiffer, The Quartermaster Corps: Organization, Supply, and Services, p. 38.

11. Around the time Dogs for Defense was dissolving in 1946, and at the outbreak of the Korean War in 1950, a small war dog program ran in the interim. This program sought to acquire the best German Shepherd breeding

stock available in Germany. Only seven bitches and one male were acquired, and this is most likely where this handful of scout dogs originated.

12. Roy E. Appleman, *Disaster in Korea: The Chinese Confront MacArthur* (Williams-Ford Texas A & M University Military History Series) (publication place: Texas A&M University Press, 1989), 1. Mr. Appleman illustrates a major source for provoking negative public opinion of the war by quoting an article in the *New York Times* by journalist Hanson Baldwin in December of 1951. Mr. Baldwin wrote, "The dangerous alternatives of another Munich or Oriental Dunkerque loomed yesterday as the Korean crisis darkened." This reference to disastrous campaigns of WWII, planted a fear of never-ending conflict in the minds of Americans. Appleman effectively makes the case that these types of articles were the norm and not the exception.

13. Lemish, 157. The 26th Infantry Scout Dog Platoon was cited in 1953 for meritorious service in battle. Different members were awarded medals by the end of the conflict to include three Silver Stars, six Bronze Stars for Valor, and multiple Bronze Stars for Meritorious Service. Only one dog, York, was awarded for service and was brought home to give demonstrations of his capabilities. He became a propaganda tool for recruitment in the years leading up to Vietnam.

14. "Information on Emotional Support Dogs," United States Dog Registry Information, 2013, usdogregistry.org (accessed October 4, 2016). Although the psychological healing abilities of dogs has always been commonly known, it has only been within the past decade that they have received recognition for those abilities by the scientific community. Emotional Support Dogs are available and protected under Federal Law (Fair Housing Amendments Act, Air Carrier Access Act, et al.) for anyone with a diagnosed mental health issue such as anxiety, depression, bipolar disorder, mood disorder, panic attacks, phobias, post-traumatic stress disorder, or suicidal thoughts/tendencies. Of course, military members can and do experience the full

gambit of these issues in battle, or on deployment, with many of them experiencing them long after they return home. Oddly, the Veteran's Administration only granted accessibility to VA facilities for veterans prescribed Emotional Support Dogs on August 17, 2015. This according to a news release issued by them on that date on their website, va.org.

15. Taken from the oral history of Leyte sailor Kent Madenwald, February 8, 2012.

16. Lemish, 151. Lemish quotes from the article "War Dogs" in *Military Review*, July 1953: "In 1949 for instance, it took an entire infantry battalion to guard several warehouses and supply depots in Japan. Yet within a four-month span, over $600,000 worth of material was lost through theft. When 125 handlers and 65 dogs took over the same guard responsibilities, not a single dollar's loss could be attributed to theft during the twelve months. This accomplishment released 600 men from guard duties, netting the government millions of dollars in savings."

17. Mark Derr, *A Dog's History of America: How Our Best Friend Explored, Conquered, and Settled a Continent* (New York: Overlook Press, 2013), 297. The Japanese obtained 25,000 Shepherds from the Germans during World War II. They were deployed with devastating effect on the people of China and Southeast Asia throughout the war. The surviving dogs were taken as spoils of war during the American occupation of Japan (1945–1951).

TWO: HARLAN

1. Navsource Online: Service Ship Photo Archive, USNS General R. L. Howze, navsource.org (August 2, 2015).

THREE: PRINZ

1. Orlean, Susan (2011). *Rin Tin Tin: The Life and the Legend*. New York City: Simon & Schuster.

2. *Meet the German Shepherd Dog. akc.org* (accessed November 13, 2015) "The German Shepherd dog does not give affection lightly and is known for his dignity and stature; it is also known as a "one-man" breed for its tendency to display serious loyalty and fidelity, especially to its owner or main caretaker."

3. Gerry took a part time job as a playground attendant to make ends meet.

4. Pharaoh was sold to Mrs. Polly (Brown) Pierce of Bangor, Maine. She was the wealthy widow of Hafford Pierce, brother of the famous painter Waldo Pierce, and she was able to offer Gerry money above the full asking price for Pharaoh. Gerry was struggling to make ends meet, on a teacher's salary, and it was an offer he couldn't refuse. Later, Pharaoh had an accident in Mrs. Brown's care when hot oatmeal was dropped on his back and permanently scarred him, making him an unlikely candidate for show. Gerry took Pharaoh back a couple of years later, however, as Mrs. Pierce had lost interest in him. Gerry sold Pharaoh again, and he would go on to a successful career as a sentry dog in the U.S. Air Force with handler Samuel Yoder.

5. "Bangor Dog Off To Take Basic Training As Sentry In U.S. Army," *Bangor Daily News*, November 20, 1953.

6. As reported by the *Bangor Daily News* in the 1953 article, "Bangor Dog Off To Take Basic Training As Sentry In U.S. Army."

FOUR: THE CALL

1. "Ft. Ord California." Ft. Ord California. Accessed February 20, 2016. http://nimst.tripod.com/cgi-bin/ftord.html. Ft. Ord's military history started in 1846 and continued until the base was closed under the Base Realignment and Closure Act in 1994. The short period of the post's basic training capacity was especially significant to veterans of Korea and Vietnam as the Army's main Infantry Training Center.

2. The Buddy System is a recruitment tool the U.S. military branches have used, through several generations, to up their recruitment numbers.

Bringing in "buddies" increases the applicant pool and gives the recruit an added measure of security as they are going into something unknown with someone comforting and familiar.

3. "Canine Sentinels" *Pacific Stars And Stripes*. PIO Hq. 24th Inf. Div. U.S. Army, n.d. By the time this article was published 1954, pilfering from the posts where canine sentries were on duty, had been reduced by 95 percent.

4. "Canine Sentinels" *Pacific Stars and Stripes* "Descendants of the famed K9 Corps of World War II, the dogs are members of the regular Army, on active duty as long as they are physically fit. They are trained at the Army Dog Training Center, Ft. Carson, Col, where they return in retirement when their tours are completed."

5. "Canine Sentinels" *Pacific Stars and Stripes*. PIO Hq. 24th Inf. Div. U.S. Army n.d.

FIVE: GETTING IN

1. Lemish, 151. From 1948-1954 the responsibility, location, and leadership of America's war-dog programs shifted at least five times. It appears that the scout dog program at Camp Carson was eventually, and literally, absorbed into the sentries. Although the U.S. Quartermasters retained their responsibility for procurement of the dogs, even up until Vietnam, the sentry dog program would be run first by the Military Police Corps and then the Chief of Army Field Services at Ft. Monroe Virginia.

2. "Historical Vignette 011–Former Chief played a part in Army Integration." U.S. Army Corps of Engineers. February 2001. Accessed April 11, 2016. usage.army.mil. Desegregation began by Executive Order 9981 in 1948. The last segregated unit was disbanded in 1954.

3. The dogs were housed in an area on the perimeter of the base known as Mary Ellen Ranch. This was the same area where mules and horses were

kept. It was the place where Fowler had worked with Jasper before coming to the scout dog unit.

4.   Horowitz, Alexandra. Inside of a Dog; What Dogs See, Smell, and Know. New York, NY: Scribner, 2009. Cognitive Psychologist, Horowitz, describes the powerful perceptions of dogs by saying that their ability arises from a combination of their attention to us and their sensory prowess. She states, "Dogs are anthropologists because they study and learn about us. They observe a meaningful part of our interaction with each other—- our attention, our focus, our gaze; the result is not that they read our minds but that they recognize and anticipate us." They dogs of the 8125th were undoubtedly anticipatory of the men in a way that even the men couldn't yet fully grasp.

5.   Paterniti, Michael. "The Dogs of War." National Geographic, June 2014, 27-53. On field patrols, the average zigzagging scout dog will cover three miles to every mile walked by the handler. Their scenting ability is 100,000 times greater than that of a human. These abilities alone make the scout dog look "smart" in comparison to the average family pet. But it is their use of these tools, refined in their work (which the dogs themselves view as play), which sets them apart. Most of these dogs had been pets previously themselves.

6.   Swenson, Judy. "Watson Man Who Served in Korea K9 Unit Believes Military Dogs Deserve More Respect." Montevideo-American News (Watson), May 27, 2010, America the Beautiful sec. Peterson tells reporter Swenson that Wolf was a great dog who was excellent at his job and deserved the utmost respect both for his work and his power. He says that Wolf just "wasn't friendly."

SIX: SECRET DEPLOYMENT

1.   "Army Ships Elite Group Of Dog Faces On Secret K-9 Mission To Far East." Seattle Daily News, August 1954. The bi-line of the article reads, "Snarling Dogs Headed For Sentry Duty Lead GI Life of Luxury."

2. Seattle Daily News, ibid.

3. Hubert, Yves. "General W. H. Gordon." Dictionary of American Fighting Ships, n.d. Accessed April 23, 2016. haze gray.org. The U.S.S. W.H. Gordon was used under the MSTS (Military Transportation Service) for the purpose of troop transport from December 1951 until being placed on inactive status, and docked in Seattle, in October of 1954. The vessel which could once hold 5500 troops was virtually empty for the men and dogs of the 8,125th. It appears that this was going to be the Gordon's last voyage before being revamped, and this is the reason this ship was chosen for a group of dirty dogs and their handlers.

SEVEN: THE MISSION

1. Swenson. ibid

ELEVEN: THE DEMONSTRATIONS

1. Riots In South Korea. British Pathe' News, 1955. News Reel via Youtube. Film footage of the riots on Wolmido Island in 1955

TWELVE: SHORT TIMERS

1. "Korean: The Korean Conflict." The United States War Dog Association, Inc. US War Dog Association, n.d. Accessed March 1, 2016. uswardogs. org. The War Dog Receiving and Holding Station at Cameron Station Virginia, was put on stand-by status on 4 May, 1954. With no new dogs coming into the program, and no new sentry dog handlers being recruited, the men knew the program was drawing to a close all together.

FOURTEEN: CALLING THE PACK

1. "Korean: The Korean Conflict." The United States War Dog Association, Inc. US War Dog Association, n.d. Accessed March 1, 2016. uswardogs. org. Ft. Carson deactivated its military working dog training, altogether, in 1957. The brief history of that decision is given in the US War Dog Association's Korean War History. "A study was made by the Office of the Deputy Chief of Staff in the latter part of 1956 to determine the cost of operating the Army Dog Training Center, Fort Carson Colo. and whether, in view of limited dog requirements the activity should continue. The Center was then being used largely for the training of Air Force dogs on a prorated cost basis. On 29 December 1956, the following decisions were announced: That the Army Dog Training Center will be discontinued prior to 30 June 1957. That no funds or personnel will be programmed for this activity in Fiscal 1958. That the Air Force be given an opportunity to take over and run the dog training operation. The Air Force decided not to conduct training operations at Fort Carson and the Center was closed as directed on I July 1957.

2. "MWD Adoption FAQs." The United States War Dog Association, Inc. US War Dog Association, n.d. Accessed March 20, 2016. uswardogs.org. The War Dog Association states, "Congressional Military Working Dog adoption law gives priority first to civilian Law Enforcement Agencies, then to prior handlers, and finally to the general public. In the event that a dog's age or fitness precludes it from being considered for Law Enforcement duties, then a former handler is most often selected. Better than 90% of former MWDs are adopted by their handlers."

3. Sypesteyn, Denise K. "Canines in Combat: Military Working Dogs." San Antonio Magazine (November 2013). Accessed April 13, 2016. www. sanantoniomag.com. Up until 1998, the Air Force Military Working Dog Program purchased dogs mainly from Germany and the Netherlands. The

Air Force ramped up their military working dog breeding program in that year in hopes of securing a good supply of homegrown MWDs and reducing our nation's reliance on Europe. By 2013 only 15% of the nation's military working dog stock were bred at Lackland Air Force Base. All branches of military service now acquire their dogs from the Air Force and all handlers, across the services, train at Lackland AFB, Texas.

AFTERWORD

1. "341st Training Squadron: Lineage," 37th Training Wing. Last modified February 21, 2016. "The Army continued to train and supply sentry dogs to Air Force units in the United States until the Sentry Dog Training Branch of the Department of Security Police Training was established at Lackland Air Force Base, Texas, in October 1958." http://www.37trw.af.mil/About/FactSheets/Display/tabid/3046/Article/670140/341st-training-squadron.aspx (accessed November 28, 2016).

2. There was a bounty on the heads of the dogs during the Vietnam War, with a cash reward for any North Vietnamese Army soldier who brought back the tattooed ear as proof. From "Vietnam," The United States War Dog Association, Inc., uswardogs.org (accessed November 29, 2016).

3. "Operation Desert Storm," The United Sates War Dog Association, Inc., uswardogs.org (accessed November 29, 2016).

4. "Smarter Than You Think: Renowned Canine Researcher Puts Dogs' Intelligence on Par with 2-Year-Old Human," American Psychological Association, August 8, 2009, http://www.apa.org/news/press/releases/2009/08/dogs-think.aspx (accessed November 29, 2016). Research also showed that a dog is capable of understanding up to 250 words and has the ability to count to five.